Gordon Matthews
AN AUSTRALIAN SON

Gordon Matthews is a career diplomat who has served in
Nigeria and Argentina. He lives in Canberra and works as a
policy officer on Pacific island issues in the Department of
Foreign Affairs and Trade.

Dear Bob,
Best wishes for a
great recovery.
Love,

Gordon Matthews
AN AUSTRALIAN SON

Richard

Jan '94

William Heinemann Australia

Published 1996 by William Heinemann Australia
a part of Reed Books Australia
22 Salmon Street, Port Melbourne, Victoria 3207
a division of Reed International Books Australia Pty Limited

Typeset in Century Old Style by Eagle Graphics
Printed and bound in Australia by Griffin Paperbacks

National Library of Australia
 cataloguing-in-publication data:

Matthews, Gordon, 1952–.
 An Australian son.

 Bibliography
 ISBN 0 85561 690 3.

 1. Matthews, Gordon, 1952– . 2. Adoptees – Australia – Biography. 1. Title.

362.8298092

*This book is dedicated to women who gave children
for adoption and to Ivy Williams.*

Some names, places and identifying information have been changed to protect the privacy of certain individuals. Nothing has been altered which compromises the integrity of the story.

This book was an act of catharsis. I wrote it to make peace with myself.

CONTENTS

'In the little world in which children have their existence ...
there is nothing so finely perceived and so finely felt
as injustice.'

CHARLES DICKENS
GREAT EXPECTATIONS, 1861

'Art is a language for interpreting who you are.
I am hunting for lost pieces of myself. Aboriginal people have
always had a vast, rich culture and I am a part of this.'

ARONE RAYMOND MEEKS
PHEASANT AND KINGFISHER, 1987

ACKNOWLEDGEMENTS

So many people have contributed generously to my book that it is difficult to know where to begin. To Michael Wood and Fernando Perez Tain, my heartfelt gratitude for their constant and uncomplaining support and also to Robyn Carter who gave generously to a stranger and provided a title. Special thanks also to Susan Provan, Don Greenlees, Naomi Steer, Janet Whiting, John Lyons, Sally Hone, Andrew Quinn, Sally Pryor, Paul Judd, Margaret Campi, Janet Matthew, Digby Jacobs, Paul Grabowsky, Nicholas Coppel, Rhys Puddicombe, Tim Menetrey, Philip Stonehouse, the Maltzahns, Martine Letts, Gordon White, David Hansen, Patrick Wolfe, Hiran Perera, Kathleen McCarthy, Francesca Beddie, Liz Camilleri, Paul Johnson and Ian Kemish.

I am grateful to my Aboriginal and Torres Strait Islander community friends, including Colin and Eleanor Bourke, Flo Grant, the late Veronica Tippett, Jirra Moore and Lorraine Decker, Benny and Yvonne Mills, Traci Williams and Harry and Jenny Williams, for their unwavering support throughout the time we have known one another.

I am indebted to David Elder, David Milne, Bill Flowers, Hedley Hatch and Cameron Lamb, ex-Changi prisoner-of-war mates of my father, who generously showed me a part of him I had never seen.

To Jennifer Byrne, my gratitude for believing in the importance of my story being told and bringing it to fruition. Sincere thanks also to Julie Pinkham and everyone else at Reed Books.

Also, my deep gratitude to the members of my two families, all of whom have enriched my life.

Thanks also to Scotch College, Melbourne, for permission to use the first verse and chorus of the 'College Song', and to Sir Archibald Glenn for permission to use his comments on Colin Healey.

The quote by Raymond Meeks from *Pheasant and Kingfisher* is courtesy of Scholastic Australia. *Took the Children Away* by Archie Roach is courtesy of Mushroom Music Pty Ltd.

Finally, I would like to thank the numerous others who have contributed in many different ways to this book.

CHAPTER 1

Magical Night

Anxiously awaiting the departure hour, the most magical night of my life began to unfold. Never had anything so momentous taken place in our house, at least not as far as I was concerned. Just when the wait became so unbearable that I imagined I might explode, Mum bundled us into overcoats and hustled us out the door. As we clambered into our old black Austin, rainclouds rumbled, the sky split open and it began to pour.

The trip in to town was only twenty minutes, but it seemed to take forever. Onwards we travelled, towards the illuminated Skipping Girl vinegar sign that remains a Melbourne landmark, and across the river which separated our leafy, middle-class world from the inner suburbs and the city beyond.

Mum betrayed her excitement with animated chatter about how our new baby brother would be waiting at the hospital. Yet again we were reminded to keep the noise down and behave properly when we arrived. In the back seat, my two sisters and I guarded an empty bassinet. We would be bringing him home tonight.

Our destination was the Queen Victoria Hospital, affectionately known as the Queen Vic, an institution which for years had welcomed thousands of eager adopting parents arriving to collect new babies. As a hospital doctor, Mum had witnessed numerous joyful departures herself. Now, for the fourth time, it was her turn to collect a baby.

Mum was one of a privileged handful of adopting mothers who knew something about the baby they would eventually receive. An honorary ante-natal medical officer, she had spoken with three of the four natural mothers of her future children while they awaited their babies' births. No doubt these women would have been astounded to learn that the doctor who spoke with compassion yet professional detachment would eventually mother their offspring.

We wound along hospital corridors, all sparkling linoleum and glossy white walls, until we found ourselves facing the viewing room. Dad wrapped his arms around my waist and hoisted me high. Interminable rows of bassinets stretched out inside.

'Look son, take a look over there,' whispered Dad in a voice edged with excitement. 'See over there. The nurses are trying to find him. Keep your eyes on them. See how they're checking the name tags. They'll have him in a minute.' A wave of excitement swept over me from head to toe. Never had I experienced such pure delight.

'Look!' exclaimed Dad suddenly. 'There he is. There's your new brother. See the one the nurse is holding up. That's our one. That's your new baby brother.' Again my eyes darted towards the back of the room. For some reason I still couldn't make him out. Where was my new brother? There seemed to be babies everywhere. 'There he is, son,' repeated Dad proudly. 'Here he comes. Can you see him? Here's your brother.' Carefully cradling Peter, a nurse moved towards us, tilting the tiny bundle forward for me to see.

Acutely aware of his precious new charge, Dad drove with

inordinate care all the way home. In the back seat, Fiona, Kay and I stared mesmerised, unable to tear our eyes away from our new baby brother for even an instant. In the front, Mum and Dad conversed earnestly, reassuring themselves that Joy would have everything ready when we arrived.

Joy was a mothercraft nurse and an integral part of our family. She lived with us. Without her, our house would never have operated smoothly. Joy's association with Mum stretched back years to when Mum had served as state commissioner for handicapped Girl Guides. A seriously ill young ward of the state battling polio, Joy so impressed Mum with her courage and determination to recover that Mum took her under her wing on a permanent basis.

'I hope she hears us turning into the drive so we get inside as quickly as possible. I don't want him getting cold,' fussed Mum unnecessarily. Mum knew better than anyone there was no cause for concern. Joy would have had everything prepared for ages. After all, this was a special event. With Peter's arrival, the family Mum and Dad had craved was finally complete.

In deference both to the rain and the magnitude of the event, Dad parked halfway up the drive alongside the front porch stairs. We only ever used the main entrance on special occasions or if a stranger happened to call. Anyone familiar with the Matthews household knew that the kitchen door facing the side path was the approved entrance for daily use.

Joy appeared at the top of the stairs the instant the car doors opened, desperate for a first glimpse of the baby. 'Just look at him, will you. Isn't he gorgeous?' she drooled, her eyes glued to the bassinet. 'Better get him straight inside.'

Crossing the hall, we entered the lounge room where an open fire banished the chill. 'At least he's not crying,' said Joy thankfully. 'We'll have him settled down in no time. Not like

Gordon when he first arrived. Will you ever forget what a pro-
duction that was?' As Joy scurried off in search of a bottle, my two
sisters and I crowded the bassinet.

My mind returned to the hospital and the series of events I had
witnessed. While I couldn't understand then the significance of
what had occurred, I knew something incredible had happened.
Somehow Peter had swapped families. He belonged with us now.

CHAPTER 2

Unspeakable Secrets

Mum had always wanted children. When she learnt to her bitter disappointment that natural children would not be possible, she immediately considered adoption. Adoption offered an ideal solution and, as a young female doctor with a professional husband, meeting the requirements appeared a formality.

Mum was also lucky for another reason. In her case the actual process of choosing a baby couldn't have been easier or more personal. Mum possessed an inside channel available to precious few: Auntie Rose. Auntie Rose had been a close school friend at Melbourne's Presbyterian Ladies College and the two women had maintained regular contact ever since. Apart from friendship they also shared professional interests. Both had pursued successful careers, Mum as a doctor, Auntie Rose as a social worker. Now, entirely by coincidence, they found themselves working together at the Queen Vic. Mum attended to mothers in the ante-natal clinic while Auntie Rose processed the interminable flow of single, pregnant women who arrived from all around the country to arrange adoptions — some even travelled from abroad.

They were different times then. In Australia in the 1950s, unmarried pregnant women received no encouragement to keep their babies. Single motherhood wasn't a viable option. The prevailing view was that single women who wound up pregnant didn't deserve their babies and had no one but themselves to blame for their predicament. Conventional wisdom deemed male involvement to be incidental. It was the woman who bore responsibility.

Fortunately, this was not the view of Auntie Rose and, under her sympathetic eye, the Queen Vic adoption program attracted considerable praise both for its efficiency and sensitivity.

Many of Auntie Rose's 'clients' were women from out of town referred to the Queen Vic by their local doctors. Usually the women phoned Auntie Rose to establish contact and finalise arrangements before travelling to Melbourne, although sometimes they arrived unannounced, suitcase in hand, and Auntie Rose would find herself asking friends to take them in.

For many, with nowhere to stay, Auntie Rose arranged accommodation with families who, in exchange for domestic assistance, provided full board and a modest salary. In this way the adoption system provided welcome cheap labour for families who would otherwise have been unable to afford home help of any kind. Other women were placed in church or government-run establishments where, traumatised and alone, they waited out the gruelling final months.

Conditions in some of the church-run maternity homes were unimaginable; how hard the women worked at cleaning and scrubbing depended on the humanity of the staff. Some homes had their own small maternity hospitals and prohibited the women from going out, except on Sundays when they were frogmarched to church. At one home all mail was censored and at another the matron banned football broadcasts after learning that the father of one woman's baby was a prominent player. At a

Roman Catholic institution the women were given saints names to use instead of their real ones.

As the birth drew near, prospective mothers were 'counselled' by a social worker to formalise the adoption of their babies as early as possible. Almost without exception they had no real choice and inevitably agreed. Abhorring the idea of women effectively being forced to surrender their babies, Auntie Rose dreaded those gut-wrenching sessions more than anything. It tugged at her heart unbearably. Years later she would confide that she never wanted a single woman she processed to surrender her baby.

'Read the form carefully and sign at the bottom if you have no further questions,' Auntie Rose would say to conclude the sessions. While careful to explain the form thoroughly, her aim was to complete the process as quickly as possible. 'What's the point in torturing yourself over an outcome you're unable to influence?' she reflected later. 'Dragging it out isn't going to change a thing.' On the contrary, it could aggravate the uncomfortable business.

In 1952, the year of my birth, signing the consent form — the integral document in the adoption process — conveyed formally a mother's intention to relinquish her baby and was irreversible. Later this was changed to allow such mothers a period of thirty days in which to reconsider their decision. Auntie Rose always reminded relinquishing mothers of their rights in this regard although at some hospitals it went unmentioned. In any case, the women were usually so traumatised that sometimes such significant information failed to register. And, despite a requirement that the person obtaining consent from the relinquishing mother swear that the woman fully understood the document to be signed, the reality was often to the contrary; many failed to appreciate they were sacrificing parental rights to their children forever.

Some women who provided consent before birth were not permitted to see their babies at all. Even the most fleeting contact was discouraged to prevent bonding between mother and child. Sometimes sheets or pillows were held up over a woman's stomach during birth; other women had their faces turned away forcibly as their babies emerged; some were even blindfolded.

Violated by this experience, thousands of Australian women returned home to try to resume normal lives, their unspeakable secrets intact.

CHAPTER 3

From Different Worlds

We four children had each arrived at our eastern suburbs home in middle-class Melbourne via this unnatural route. Although you couldn't pinpoint precisely what it was, the instant you laid eyes on us, you knew we hadn't emerged from a common source. Physically, there was something obviously different about our appearances that suggested we'd been plucked randomly off the street and flung together. By any benchmark, we were an unlikely crew.

I, the eldest, was skinny and curly haired with olive skin and striking blue eyes. My eyes were unarguably my most impressive feature — people were forever commenting on them. As I grew older and came to understand the meaning of adoption, I assumed instinctively that my eye colour originated with my birth mother. She had been a fair-skinned woman from Sydney who had travelled to Melbourne to have her baby at the Queen Vic. Later, during my teenage years, Mum would recall my birth mother as possessing a broad brow and an open and gentle face. According to Auntie Rose, my natural father had been a student at Sydney

University, studying agricultural science or something like that. The precise details remained unclear.

Fiona was next, and the two of us could scarcely have appeared more dissimilar. With fair skin and chestnut hair, Fiona was like every other kid in the neighbourhood: unmistakably Anglo-Saxon.

For three and a half months of the year — between Fiona's birthday in early March and mine in the second half of June — my sister and I shared the same age. After that, once again I would leap a year ahead. The fact that the age difference between us was only eight and a half months attracted considerable attention from schoolmates and friends, especially as the two of us grew older and the duration of pregnancies became better understood.

Like me, Fiona had a previous life which had similarly shrunk from view although the odd snippet was known about her origins. As far back as I could remember, Mum had indicated that Fiona's mother had travelled from Adelaide to Melbourne to have her baby. However, I don't recall either Mum or Dad ever referring to Fiona's father. Still, that wasn't surprising if you were adopted because no one ever seemed to know anything tangible about your father. Just like mine, Fiona's father had vanished. Nothing was known about him whatsoever.

The third arrival in the family was Kay. She was everybody's favourite. Gentle and unhurried, even animals were visibly at ease around her. Kay inspired unqualified trust. Physically, she was different again. With a light complexion and blonde hair, people often assumed that her origins were Scandinavian or German. According to Auntie Rose, Kay's father had been Latvian or Lithuanian, although she wasn't precisely sure which. My understanding was that Kay's mother was a Melbourne woman, although I never really knew why. It was simply a belief I had acquired along the way. The physical contrast between Kay and myself was so striking that years later, backpacking around Asia, despite the absence of a ring and the fact that her passport referred to her as Miss and not as Mrs, people everywhere asked whether or not she was my wife.

Finally, there was Peter. Fair-skinned and chubby, his nose and cheeks freckled, my brother was uncomplicated and easygoing. The kind of youngster nobody minded having around. Travelling in Scotland years later, Mum was struck by the number of boys who reminded her of Peter when young. Unusually, it was Peter's birth mother who had disappeared from view. Mum believed my brother's father had been a marine engineer although she wasn't sure from where. Before knowing that, I had incorrectly developed the idea that Peter's father had been a Melbourne businessman. Reflecting back, I couldn't recall either Mum or Auntie Rose ever referring to Peter's mother. She was the only one of our four birth mothers whom Mum hadn't examined in the hospital.

Of the four of us, the only two with any physical similarity were Peter and Fiona. Seeing them together, one might have accepted they did in fact belong. Not because they looked especially alike, rather that they didn't appear excessively dissimilar. Undeniably Anglo-Saxon in appearance, both were obviously different to Kay and me. We had all arrived from decidedly different worlds.

This was how the Matthews family came into being. In terms of where we began our lives and how we came to constitute a family, the unlikely ingredients we shared were only Mum, Dad, Auntie Rose and the Queen Vic, along with our respective natural mothers who, for whatever reason, had decided to give us away.

CHAPTER 4

Mum and Dad

My mother is an extraordinary woman by any measure. At a time when women's lives were expected to revolve around home and children, and the notion of a middle-class woman in employment attracted disapproval, Mum determined her own agenda. She studied for six years to qualify as a doctor, then embarked on a full-time and successful career in medicine. Joy and other mothercraft nurses lived with us to assist during those early years, although Mum devoted all her free time to the family. Later, in her seventies, as well as serving on a plethora of boards and committees, Mum would complete a masters degree in psychological medicine and a fine arts major, counsel women suffering from post-natal depression, and try to improve conditions for female prisoners who mothered their children inside. We admired our mother's achievements a great deal.

And we weren't alone. Her warmth and humility attracted almost everyone. Her infrequently made-up face reflected the inner peace and contentment which I grew to appreciate and envy more than any other quality about her, although her ability to avoid and ignore anything negative or upsetting was sometimes maddening as well. Childhood was precious to Mum, and despite her best intentions, she did not prepare us as well as she might have for the real world we would confront as adults. Decades later, that would be the only criticism we children shared of our mother's efforts at raising us.

Simplicity and honesty were also apparent in Mum's dress. Apart from the comfort they provided, Mum considered clothes unimportant. Our mother was a large woman and fashion and style were inconsequential. After all, you didn't judge someone by how they looked or what they did. We were taught, as far back as I can remember, it is who they are that is important. Unassuming in every aspect of her life, Mum abhorred affectation, snobbishness and unhelpful criticism of any kind. She focused on what was good and positive in a person, forgiving or rationalising any shortcomings and mistakes. Everyone possessed positive qualities and each life held intrinsic value. From Mum's perspective, there wasn't a single individual who didn't possess something of incalculable worth.

In contrast with Mum, Dad was slight in stature with receding silver hair that sprouted more sparsely as we grew older. We kids shrieked with laughter at the absurdity of Dad heading off to the barber to have a trim. Amiable, without a malicious bone in his body, Dad was reserved and rarely spoke unnecessarily. Fiona always described him as a thorough gentleman in every sense. Despite irreparable damage to his heart as a prisoner-of-war of the Japanese, my father stayed fit by seizing opportunities to walk whenever they arose. Sporting shorts and one of the Hawaiian shirts he obtained during a visit to Honolulu in the 1950s, I picture him vividly now, striding purposefully along the beach where we spent our school holidays, the four of us struggling to maintain pace with his sturdy athletic legs. Dad was also emotionally damaged by the war. Countless times I wondered what had caused him to seal off his feelings so tightly. He rarely relaxed completely and just let go.

To captive young ears like ours, nothing beat snuggling up on the lounge-room couch for one of Dad's Changi yarns. Some of them filled us with horror. One which left a particularly strong impression concerned a group of soldiers who, after being captured while attempting to break out of the camp, found themselves marched to a nearby beach where they were executed slowly by firing squad from the feet up. Defiantly refusing to die, one of the soldiers had glared contemptuously at his assassins as they pumped bullets into him. Stories like that made us clamour for more. 'Go on Dad, just one more,' we would plead, desperate for one final story before being unceremoniously shunted off to bed. Sometimes we played soldiers ourselves, striding around the lounge room to the accompaniment of an Elgar march blaring from the gramophone.

There were also Dad's Mosquito Squad yarns, tales about the small band of men responsible for identifying and destroying malarial mosquito breeding grounds both inside and around the camp. Accompanied by a Korean guard, the squad would search out mosquito breeding places and collect suspect larvae which Dad would then analyse. If infection was confirmed, the oilers launched an offensive, spraying oil across the water to suffocate the disease-carrying offenders, or performed draining operations. Since bags were never searched, these excursions outside provided an ideal opportunity to gather fallen ripe coconuts before land crabs gnawed into them. Squad members rapidly became adept at shredding the husk and grating the kernel for use in pap, the porridge produced from polished rice ground into powder, which was served up daily.

Even more fascinating than Dad's yarns was his impressive

display of war wounds. Dad's heart condition saw him rushed to hospital periodically, the ambulance siren shrieking wildly. As far as I was concerned, Dad's heart attacks outdid just about anything. Not only was there the chaos of the moment, there were also myriad side-benefits: casseroles from the neighbours; the visitors who bestowed atmosphere upon the house; and the respite from daily routine. In a way it rankled that Dad wasn't taken to hospital more often. As a youngster it never crossed my mind that he might not, in fact, return.

In addition to his heart condition, Dad displayed other war-related ailments. A nail-less toe, the legacy of a thrust from a Japanese rifle butt on the Changi parade ground, particularly fired my imagination. After Dad recounted what had happened, I couldn't keep my eyes away whenever the celebrated toe appeared in view, imagining the rifle butt crashing down painfully. Dad's skin cancers also attracted attention. He seemed to be forever heading off to the doctor to have slivers nicked from his long-suffering ears.

Mum and Dad first met as second-year science students at a Melbourne University botany lecture in 1937, shortly before an Anglocentric Australia celebrated the coronation of King George VI, with war clouds already apparent to some. My mother also studied medicine, however neither science nor medicine had been her first choice. Veterinary science had been her preferred option but it was available only in Sydney and Pop and Gran Brodrick had been unwilling to permit their seventeen-year-old daughter to study interstate alone.

Mum first noticed Dad seated in the row behind her chatting animatedly on the unlikely subject of spiders. Although Mum didn't share Dad's interest, she was attracted by the resonance of his voice. From then on every afternoon, accompanied by a friend, my mother would wait on a bench, strategically located between the anatomy and zoology schools, for my father to appear to commence his journey home. As he passed, Dad would raise his hat and initiate conversation. 'Good afternoon Miss Brodrick,' he would say. 'Good afternoon Mr Matthews,' Mum would reply. With that simple ritual, her day would be made.

Another technique of Mum's was to scour zoology textbooks in search of questions sufficiently difficult to justify a phone call to Dad for assistance. The two of them would chat endlessly, while Big Gran and Mum's sister Phil ferried assistance: a stool, a knee-rug, hot cocoa in winter, home-made lemonade in summer, anything that might enhance my mother's efforts.

Mum and Dad married in 1946, soon after Dad returned from the war. Not long afterwards they purchased what was to be our only family home from old friends of Pa and Gran Matthews who felt deeply about Dad's suffering as a prisoner-of-war. Dad found work at the Herald and Weekly Times where Pa Matthews was also employed. When Dad retired after writing more than one thousand weekly gardening columns for the *Herald*, his departure concluded a continuous family association with the paper stretching more than fifty years — the longest uninterrupted family link in the paper's history.

While recently qualified doctors and journalists clearly earned more than many, post-war salaries didn't stretch all that far. Mum fashioned makeshift curtains from unbleached calico and the two of them perched on boxes throughout their first year of married life. Chairs were an unaffordable luxury. The neighbourhood in which our parents chose to raise their family was uncompromisingly Anglo-Saxon, a place of clearly defined values which were staunchly adhered to by families who remained for decades. Untainted by discord, it was difficult to imagine anywhere more predictable, safe or secure.

Residents of the brick end of the street, our single-storey house, constructed in the 1930s like several others, fronted vacant railway land, referred to affectionately as 'the tip'. We children lived on 'the tip', our private Arcadia, and it was there that much of childhood unfolded. Our end of the street was referred to as the brick end to distinguish it from its weatherboard counterpart which featured smaller, more modest timber houses exclusively. Although this division remained unimportant throughout primary school years, by secondary school, brick-enders all attended one of the nearby private schools. In contrast, the weatherboard-enders generally enrolled in either the local high school or, if they wished to pursue a trade instead of a profession, a technical school.

The only outsiders to disturb this neat and tranquil world were Italians who escaped the inner suburbs on Sundays to picnic and harvest the wild fennel which flourished across from our house. Perched on the front fence, the four of us would observe entranced as the fennel was gathered. From our perspective fennel was a weed. How anyone could eat it we couldn't begin to imagine. Our cultural horizons didn't stretch anywhere near that far. It wasn't until later, when the first wave of post-war immigrants abandoned the inner suburbs for neighbourhoods like ours, that an Indian family arrived to herald the advent of a new and transformed Australia.

CHAPTER 5

The Chosen Baby

It must have been before first grade that Mum and Dad introduced me to *The Chosen Baby*, a syrupy tale which explained adoption. It was the most special story I'd ever heard.

'Come on, tea's over now. You promised you'd read to us,' Fiona and I would plead, desperate to hear the story that enchanted us. Luckily Kay and Peter were still a bit too young, which meant that Fiona and I were able to monopolise our parents' reading time. Usually it was Dad who read, the two of us perched contentedly on his knees. We always made him read slowly so that we could savour every word.

The purpose of the book was to explain adoption to young children and, with regular reprints since its initial publication decades earlier, *The Chosen Baby* had proved an unqualified success. Mr and Mrs Brown were the main protagonists in the story. I loved hearing how the Browns had provided a home for not one but two special adopted babies. Even though to begin with I didn't fully understand the precise difference between an 'adopted' baby and a regular baby, the process of adoption sounded exciting. The Browns' preference was for a baby boy, although if that wasn't possible, a little girl was fine too. What really mattered was to obtain a baby somehow.

One particular illustration depicted the Browns chatting with a woman named Mrs White in her office, questioning the ins and outs of actually obtaining a baby. Another depicted Mrs White visiting the Browns' home to find out if it was a suitable place for a special adopted baby to live.

After what seemed an interminably long period, since everyone wanted a baby, the telephone finally rang. It was Mrs White, asking the Browns to come straight over to look at a baby boy she hoped might prove suitable. Racing outside, the Browns hailed a passing taxi and headed for Mrs White's office. Luckily for them, Mrs White's instincts were spot on. The Browns fell in love with the baby boy the instant they laid eyes on him, taking him home with them the very next morning.

The story went on to explain how the Browns subsequently found a sister for Peter, their new baby boy. Now with a boy and a girl and their family complete, the Browns couldn't have been happier. Things had turned out perfectly.

Sometimes Dad embellished the story or tailored it for Fiona and me individually in order to explain how each of us had been selected. Our favourite part was when Dad explained that other parents had not been nearly as lucky as he and Mum because they hadn't been able to handpick their children. They'd had to accept what they'd been given. The way Dad made it sound, adoption was a privilege bestowed on precious few. The story made me feel enormously special. I too was 'The Chosen Baby'.

And so in this way adoption was introduced, entering each of our lives entirely naturally, unlike in some families where adoptees were told they were natural children. I am unable to recall a time when I was not conscious of my adoption, this enigmatic kernel of my existence. Only later would it have such an unforeseen influence on whom and what I would become. While proud of being adopted and the distinctiveness which it conferred, my circumstances also gave rise to embarrassment. Not on a scale to warrant mention to Mum and Dad, nor in a way that precipitated concern, rather it stemmed from an inexplicable belief that while normal and nothing to be ashamed of, adoption was not something to advertise or boast about unnecessarily. Similarly, adoption was never a subject which attracted regular discussion around the meal table although Mum and Dad would have viewed that as entirely normal.

Adoption was something to share with a close friend, a primary school secret for a select, privileged few. Anyway, who would ever have understood? Adoption was a difficult concept for a regular child to comprehend. How did you explain that your birth mother loved you so much that she gave you away? How did you explain that you lived with people you called parents but who were not your own flesh and blood, and that four sets of natural parents were responsible for creating your particular family? That was difficult enough for me to understand much less convey to anyone else. If you belonged to a normal family, then how could you grasp what it was like to be born into circumstances akin to mine. When I considered it, Mum and Dad were right. I was different. Already there was something which defined me as essentially on my own.

I had no idea how my brother and sisters felt about their adoption whatsoever. While treated openly within the family, adoption was something we never really discussed although on the odd occasion each of us did separately with Mum and Dad. Instead, we each dealt with the fact of our adoption in a private and personal way. As in many Australian households of the era, what you really thought and felt about personally was broached only superficially, never openly and honestly. In some respects I attributed this to Dad, with what the war had inflicted and the emotional barriers the Changi experience had erected.

Early on I sensed the importance of adoption in Fiona's conception of things. I felt certain she wondered who her natural mother was and why she had given her away. Like me, she was acutely aware of originating somewhere else, somewhere different. On one occasion, after informing friends of her adoption who had reacted sceptically to the fact, Fiona returned home to seek reassurance and confirmation of what she knew undoubtedly to be true. Confirmation was important to Fiona. It was fundamental to her security. On another occasion, when she was only four years of age, I'd asked what it meant to be adopted. 'It means you've got two mothers,' Fiona had blurted out before Mum and Dad had a chance to reply.

By comparison, it was difficult to determine how Kay felt about her special status. Tranquil and self-contained, she exuded a serenity similar to Mum. Perhaps growing up in the same household as her two older siblings, more volatile and therefore distinctly different, had something to do with it. Kay managed everything in her own mild-mannered way, rarely speaking stridently about anything until considerably older. If adoption was prominent in her world, then she certainly held it close to her heart. I never knew if my sister dwelt on where she had sprung from or contemplated the woman who had given her life, although I imagined she probably did. Kay was too sensitive not to have done so, even if only sporadically. As a mother in her forties, I imagine my sister contemplated adoption far more keenly although I couldn't be entirely sure because it was one of the few things we never discussed with total candour. I had read accounts by adopted women who claimed that the birth of their own children had acted as a catalyst for initiating searches for their natural mothers. These women had confronted an overwhelming desire to know where they came from so they could inform their offspring.

Of the four of us, the one least concerned with being adopted was Peter. He rarely alluded to the fact of his adoption, and then only in a matter-of-fact, dismissive kind of way, which suggested adoption barely figured in his conception of himself. If Peter's outside appearance provided any indication, then my brother's attitude to his adoption was unequivocal. As far as he was concerned, his natural mother had chosen to give him away; Mum and Dad were now his parents, and that was the end of the story. Essentially there was nothing else to consider. Peter's sense of family, his notion of himself, and of where he fitted in the overall scheme of things, was crystal clear. His identity was based entirely on where he existed now. For him there was no sense of having originated elsewhere, no compelling mystery demanding investigation. For Peter, life commenced with Mum and Dad. It was as simple as that.

Sometimes I wondered if my brother genuinely believed what he espoused or if his position was assumed for self-protection, because the occasional discrepancy did arise, albeit rarely. Once, in secondary school, Peter had returned home irritated that some of his mates had refused to believe he was adopted. Peter had asked Mum to write a letter for him to verify the truth of his claim. Like Fiona, on this sole occasion, Peter had required confirmation. Instead Mum had suggested that if any of my brother's peers wished to contact her directly, then she would be more than willing to speak with them.

Perhaps contemplating where he might have originated was too confrontational and difficult for Peter to deal with. Maybe that was why he appeared to shove adoption aside. Whatever the case, I doubted he ever wondered about any aspect of his natural mother or the circumstances which she must have encountered, certainly never seriously. 'I've only got one mother,' Peter would proclaim with an assurance impossible to dissuade. My view contrasted entirely because I had believed, ever since learning I was adopted, that none of our mothers had chosen to surrender us willingly and each had confronted a dilemma of unimaginable proportions. It was an idea that had evolved entirely naturally. No woman with an open range of choices surrendered a baby because she wanted to. Who seriously believed that? From my perspective, my brother's attitude was unfathomable.

CHAPTER 6

An Unusual Household

Mum and Dad's recipe for running the house violated just about every established rule. In those days, virtually no one accepted the notion of a mother of four working full time. The principal bread winner of the family, Mum despised housework more than anything. Instead, she pursued her own undomestic agenda single-mindedly. Dad's flexible work arrangements as an agricultural and horticultural journalist meant he could combine his professional life with managing a household. That suited Mum down to the ground. Without Dad's assistance, she could never have done all the things she wanted to do.

In time, Dad ceased working a regular day at the *Herald* in order to concentrate fully on his expanding role as house husband. Rising punctually at six, he commenced his day with the unenviable task of coaxing us from our beds and arranging breakfast. On weekday mornings Mum departed first, Dad farewelling her ceremoniously from the front porch in his dressing gown, before hurrying back inside to organise the rest of us off to school. That taken care of, he then headed for the Herald and Weekly Times to prepare his articles.

When it came to work, Dad was a bit of a star. Highly regarded in his field, he was easily the best-known gardening expert in Victoria, providing advice on facets of his field from soil chemistry and gardenia bed drainage to garlic sprays and allaying gardeners' fears about wasps in tree ferns. The four of us always swelled with pride when teachers at school or the parents of friends sought advice about particular gardening problems. Familiar with the headshot that accompanied his articles, readers even accosted Dad in the supermarket. Imagining something spectacular, some even asked if they could visit to view our own garden first-hand. We found those requests hilarious because our garden was unexceptional. Apart from some roses on which he lavished attention and the silver birch which dominated the front garden, there was nothing that warranted particular attention. Dad never possessed the strength necessary to transform the garden into something special.

Dad also received a steady stream of enquiries and fan mail, all of which received individual and considered attention. He spent hours dealing with them all. 'So Rodney Matthews is your father?' people would comment, almost reverently. Most Melbourne households purchased the *Herald* which meant tens of thousands of readers were familiar with Dad's regular Thursday supplements. Of the thousands of letters he received over the years, the ones which uplifted Dad the most were those from lonely people who said he had found them new friends in their gardens.

Preparation of the evening meal and household shopping were other integral items on Dad's agenda. Dad enjoyed shopping because it was something he never attacked in one fell swoop, adopting instead a more piecemeal approach by visiting the supermarket several times weekly to top up supplies. Shopping lay strictly within Dad's domain. Mum never went near the supermarket although she did take us to buy school uniforms and other necessities at the outset of each school year. Likewise she never missed ferrying us into town to view the Myer Christmas windows and meet Father Christmas upstairs at Foys.

While accompanying Dad on his supermarket excursions certainly had disadvantages, it was definitely preferable to homework, and with practice the four of us developed into competent shoppers. Given Dad's proclivity to purchase the same items, this wasn't all that spectacular an achievement. It didn't take long to discover exactly where relevant items resided and what needed to be extracted from the shelves. Sometimes the four of us would play memory games, tearing around the aisles to establish who was most familiar with their contents. Fiona usually came out the winner.

Without question the most boring part of supermarket excursions was returning home to unpack and store our purchases. We detested unloading the supermarket bags from the station wagon, which had replaced our Austin, and lugging them inside.

Like any committed housewife, Dad was a stickler for detail. Each item boasted its own special place. Regular items included lamb chops, boston buns and massive quantities of canned creamed rice. Having acquired a taste for rice in Malaya and Singapore, Dad was addicted to the stuff. The rest of us considered it the pits. 'Not more creamed rice,' the four of us would groan as the sago-like mush appeared yet again, accompanied by canned fruit. Given how often Dad had been forced to consume rice during his war years, I would have thought it would be the last thing to take his fancy. But there were cartons of the stuff stowed around the kitchen.

Unfortunately, the predictability evident in Dad's shopping also characterised his culinary endeavours. As in most Australian households, meat and vegetables represented standard weeknight fare. These were the dying days of White Australia but Asian influences were not yet apparent. Still there was no getting around the fact that ours was the only house I ever encountered in which the father prepared the evening meal. So Dad earned points, despite his repetitious fare.

Routinely, every afternoon around five, my father donned an apron. That was when you made yourself scarce because it was then that Dad rounded up loiterers to assist. Everything needed to be dished up well before 'Bellbird', the popular television series about life in a country town, commenced on weekday evenings. Once 'Bellbird' began, all else ground to an uncompromising halt.

Dishing up dinner was preceded by another essential task: the preparation of Mum's home-from-work cup of tea. That ritual involved placing tea leaves in a pot beside a gently boiling kettle at around six every evening. With that taken care of and dinner underway, all that remained was Mum's appearance at the door. Sometimes we would compete to see who could hear her first before rushing to alert Dad. 'Quick, she's coming. Pour the water now,' we would yell while tearing down the side path to assist Mum inside with her bags.

As Mum struggled wearily up the path, Dad poured the water for her cuppa which was accepted gratefully as she sank into her favourite lounge-room chair. While Mum unwound in front of the television and an appetising smell wafted through the house accompanied by cries from the kitchen and the clang of pots and pans, Dad and his assistants finalised preparations. Mum would never have survived without her regular doses of junk television. No matter how much the rest of us rubbished them, Mum defended her favourite programs vigorously. 'They're just what I need after work,' she would declare unapologetically, refusing to be intimidated by the rest of us. 'The last thing I need is to have to think. If it's not mindless I'm not interested,' she would insist.

Reflecting on Mum's day, it wasn't difficult to understand precisely what she meant. By the time she arrived home, Mum just wanted to switch off from her demanding job as child welfare officer, later chief medical officer for the Melbourne City Council, with responsibility for the city's health services and a department comprising more than two hundred individuals. When the time arrived for Dad to dish up dinner, Mum was always so exhausted that she accepted Dad's offerings with a compliance that baffled the rest of us completely. Mum enjoyed simple food. She couldn't have cared less what Dad placed in front of her.

Friday night was far and away the highlight of our week. Friday meant 'Friday Surprise' and a respite from Dad's cooking in the form of fish and chips or takeaway Chinese from the local East Kew shops. To cap things off, Mum would stop at the local milk bar on her way home to obtain something as Friday Surprise for that particular week. Hovering like vultures, the four of us would loiter expectantly, anxious for Mum to appear over the horizon. Drawing up kerbside, Mum would be confronted by cries for Twisties, Fags, Choo Choo Bars, Cherry Ripes or perhaps a special treat from Darrell Lea purchased in the city. We became incredibly adept at relieving Mum of her bags the instant she emerged from the car. That way we could hustle her inside and extract Friday Surprise with ease. Waiting until tea was over was out of the question as far as we were concerned and, thankfully, Mum and Dad usually didn't appear to mind.

CHAPTER 7

The Question of Colour

Although incidents occurred long before I could begin to remember, as far back as I can recall people began to enquire about my skin colour and racial background. Observing me in my bassinet at around six months of age, Pop Brodrick would refer to me affectionately as his 'little Abo', despite stern chastisement from Mum. Anglocentric and white as snow, Pop's generation could discern a touch of the tar brush instinctively, so it was unsurprising that my grandfather perceived my racial difference long before it had even occurred to anyone else. On another occasion, Mum had visited her family at their Melbourne bayside home. 'Give my love to my little Abo,' Pop had pronounced as my mother prepared to leave. Mum had reacted angrily. Farewelling my mother at the door, her sister Phil returned to the sun room where my grandfather was seated, and asked precisely what he had meant. Pop explained that he had always thought that I had colour and that I was probably Aboriginal. 'It's the most likely conclusion, isn't it?' Pop had stated matter-of-factly. Pop was a sensitive man who adored us all, but direct and cut and dry in his views. For him what he had said had been a natural, unexceptional thing to say, certainly not meant to be hurtful.

During those early years, the mothercraft nurses who lived with us, kindergarten teachers, relatives and visitors to the house, also made references, never unkind or broadcast widely, but significant enough to influence the childhood landscape which I inhabited. Primary school friends commented similarly, likening me good-naturedly to the golliwogs which they cherished before political correctness banished them a generation later. In this context, it was unsurprising that when a family friend announced she was to travel abroad, I requested a black baby as a present. My disappointment was acute when I received black silk pyjamas instead.

While nothing occurred more significant than this, my developing sense of difference, of having originated elsewhere, was reinforced considerably. Not only was I different by virtue of my adoption, now there was something else of far greater import, blatantly visible and impossible to ignore. A seed had been sown. My difference was now confirmed on two levels. Colour had surfaced as something significant, a defining and meaningful attribute, one which had penetrated imperceptibly the essence of who I was.

My siblings were also aware of my colour and of how it distinguished me from them, although, like adoption, it was alluded to only infrequently, usually by Fiona. She was perceptive and keenly attuned to our family's difference. Fiona felt even more intensely than me the fact that we had all arrived from somewhere else. Like Pop she could sense my racial difference. Although Kay and Peter were aware of that too, for them it didn't represent anything especially significant. They were younger, contented and relaxed, both in relation to themselves as individuals and the universe in which they lived. The fact that their brother was darker was not of notable importance.

From my own perspective, while never acknowledging it openly, I confronted my difference every time I examined myself in a mirror or studied our family photos, especially following summer holidays, invariably spent at the beach. There I would be, in stark contrast with my siblings: long skinny legs, unruly curly hair, my stomach protruding from a slightly swayed back, and that mysterious olive skin which originated no one knew where. Unlike my brother and sisters, I didn't turn pink and peel. My skin absorbed the sun naturally, as friend rather than foe. My summer colour was also something of which I was intensely proud, despite ruminating privately over its possible source, this element of my existence shared with no other individual in my world. On one occasion my colour won me a radio station contest for the darkest suntan on the beach. 'You're as black as an Abo,' quipped the announcer off-air. When summer ended, I was always inexplicably brown in comparison with others, a gleaming bronze nugget, striking and enigmatic, a youngster with origins in a different, more exotic world.

My racial difference was, however, largely ignored. In our Anglocentric environment it would have been indiscreet and inappropriate for anyone to refer to or make an issue of my apparent difference. That would have been disruptive, unjustifiable, and provoked discomfort all round. In any case, why would anyone choose to do that when for all intents and purposes I was a happy, well-adjusted youngster coasting along contentedly in the world where I had landed.

So unbeknown to others, awareness of colour was already ignited inside me, incandescent and burning brightly, part of my inner landscape, which no one ever probed. It was a strange thing, my skin. After all, how many children focused on or preoccupied themselves with colour? I doubted that any youngster did that, certainly not in our world. Not even coloured children dwelt on that aspect of themselves because, unless they had been removed from their parents, their colour was dealt with in context, linked inextricably to parents and siblings, it wasn't something which generated concern or enquiry. For children whose colour was experienced in that setting, colour wasn't a catalyst for speculation, certainly not at that early stage. They knew who they were and every aspect of themselves added up. The picture was complete. Colour didn't equate with difference.

In these early years, I had no real idea if my colour was an aspect of me which Mum and Dad contemplated consciously. Other than the occasional comment from others, which no one ever dwelt on and usually passed ignored, there was no indication that colour had surfaced as an issue of significance for them. Later Mum would tell me that at that early stage of my life, my colour was something she never really noticed. Mum wouldn't have cared about colour anyway. Her thoughts were bound up with the joy of having children. Mum never thought of any of us as other than delightful infants to whom a smattering of what had been learnt in life could be magically passed on. She was never really conscious of my colour distinguishing me although by the time secondary school arrived things had changed considerably. In any case an olive tinge was natural to Mum. She viewed my father's complexion as slightly olive, a legacy of his southern English ancestry, traceable to Spanish sailors shipwrecked on the Cornish coast. Accordingly, colour was an integral element of my mother's perception of my father, albeit one which I doubted anyone else shared, least of all me.

In relation to Dad, I had no idea whatsoever what he thought about my colour and racial background. I didn't know if he pondered it at all. During secondary school, when I experienced racial taunts, I still didn't know what he thought. Certainly colour was something we never discussed.

Years later, Auntie Phil recounted how once, observing me as a youngster on the beach, she had been struck sufficiently by my colour to ask about it for the very first time. 'What do you think Gordon's racial background is?' she had enquired of my father beside her.

'Pacific islander,' Dad had replied.

Auntie Phil surmised the same. 'I saw palm trees every time I looked at you,' she would inform me as an adult.

Likewise it was never a subject that surfaced in discussion with my siblings, perhaps because we all consciously ignored it. Colour was not an issue for the family or public arena. This was the 1950s in white, middle-class Australia. To have focused on it would have rocked the boat and we were brought together by Auntie Rose to be a contented, harmonious family.

CHAPTER 8

Dear Abo

On 10 August 1962, Dad announced proudly that Mum had won a scholarship to study for a Diploma of Child Health at London University. Although Mum was over the moon, she only accepted the scholarship on the proviso that her employer, the Melbourne City Council Health Department, permit the family to accompany her. It all sounded too exciting for words. The romance of foreign places had already infiltrated our lives because, as horticultural editor of the *Herald*, Dad had travelled overseas, preparing articles for the paper about his experiences and the gardens he'd visited. The four of us eagerly awaited the postcards he sent from exotic destinations and my treasured childhood possessions included the Indian buffalo skin jacket which returned with him from Canada.

On this occasion it was decided that Dad would take a year off work in order to continue his established role as house husband. I could barely contain my excitement as Dad explained how in one year to the day we would depart for England on the P&O liner *Chusan*. For a ten-year-old Australian boy, in an age when few people travelled, the idea of heading off to the other side of the world seemed the ultimate in childhood adventures. Never having encountered anyone fortunate enough to have done anything vaguely as exciting, I reckoned I must have been the luckiest kid in the world.

Exactly one year after Dad's announcement, we were ceremoniously farewelled by the neighbours who delivered a speech and presented us with a travel rug. There was a strong sense of community and affection between households where we lived. We were always in one another's homes and closely involved. Amid exhortations to send postcards and fevered excitement, we packed into Pop Brodrick's Ford and headed for Station Pier to rendezvous with Dad's relatives for one final farewell.

Apart from Dad's younger brother and his family who were closer to our ages, we weren't nearly as close to Dad's side of the family as we were to the Brodricks, even though all the Matthews came to farewell us. I never believed that we four children were ever considered true family by the Matthews in the complete sense, certainly not by Dad's mother, a conservative, narrow-minded woman who disliked Labor supporters and Roman Catholics, and whose outstanding cooking represented one of her few redeeming features. Despite presents for Christmas and birthdays, and our inclusion on family occasions, we remained outsiders, never made to feel as though we truly belonged.

With the Brodricks, the situation was dramatically different. Although Pop and Gran were traditional and would have adored natural grandchildren, there was never any suggestion that we were other than fully fledged family. Eager anticipation surrounded visits to our grandparents' bayside home, furnished tastefully with antiques and objects from Gran's side of the family, the scent from my grandmother's lavender bed permeating the entire front garden, and the beach close by where seagulls tussled and cantankerously over scraps. Pop and Gran were content beside the sea.

The death of Mum's brother Warren, killed in his mid-twenties in a plane crash during the war, cast a shadow over my mother's family of which I was always aware. After that disaster, Pop displayed his grief openly, wearing only black ties and shoes in remembrance of his son, who like Mum had graduated as a doctor. Usually Pop wore suits, brown pinstripes or grey, a rose through his button-hole, his father's watch chain suspended from his waistcoat. Following his death, the chain would be the only possession of my grandfather's that I would request as a keepsake.

For Gran Brodrick, I always sensed that I helped in some small way to relieve the loss of her son. We adored Gran Brodrick, who lived an extraordinary 104 years. Occasionally when I was older, the two of us alone together, Gran would refer to her son and tell me how fine he had been. 'Why did God do that to me? Why did he take my boy,' she would demand in anguish, grief and indignation transforming her face, while my throat ached and I struggled to hold back tears.

During our month-long voyage to England — which included stops in Singapore, Penang, Bombay, Aden, Port Said and Naples — we abandoned the correspondence school work which Mum had arranged for us prior to departing Melbourne. Shipboard life provided myriad activities of infinitely greater interest including water sports and deck games. My first taste of life outside Australia was the sight of fishing junks in Singapore harbour on a humid tropical dawn. That morsel redefined the parameters of the world in which I lived. Everything was so exotic and I was hungry to experience it all.

In Singapore, Dad conducted a pilgrimage to Changi, the scene of his suffering twenty years earlier. It was an enormously special day for Dad as he confronted ghosts from the past. We children felt extremely privileged standing next to him while he talked with the British guard on duty. The prison felt uncannily familiar after a lifetime of Dad's stories. In a way I considered myself privy to some of the secrets hidden behind its walls.

Following our arrival at Southampton and a journey by train up to London, we established ourselves temporarily in Earls Court, known commonly as Kangaroo Valley, while Dad searched for somewhere permanent to live. Mum was struck by the number of West Indians, who like us congregated around stands to buy coffee and hotdogs in the evening. English society was in the throes of transformation, the legacy of its colonial past, already altered significantly from Mum's rarefied perceptions of how the country would be. Shortly after we moved into the semi-detached, two-storey house in East Barnet, Hertfordshire, in London's northern environs, where we spent the duration of our stay. Cramped by Australian standards, it was impressive in the eyes of my English school friends.

From an eleven-year-old's perspective, our arrival in England fortuitously coincided with Beatlemania. Quite a few classmates acquired Beatles haircuts although for some reason Beatles boots were banned. Instead we all wore chisel-toed shoes which were considered to be cool. This was the year 'She Loves You' — the first single I ever purchased — topped the charts for an unheard of six months. No one discussed anything except the four Liverpudlians who released their second LP, *With the Beatles*, on the day John F. Kennedy was assassinated; an event I learned about from the morning newspaper before returning inside to inform Mum, who was seated on the toilet stowed under the stairs. That year, 1963, also saw the Searchers, Gerry and the Pacemakers, The Merseybeats, Cilla Black — a favourite of Dad's — and many others launched from England's industrial heartland to international stardom. The same year Margaret Smith (later

Court) became the first Australian to win the Wimbledon women's singles title, a crown which she forfeited the following year to Brazil's Maria Bueno despite my courtside barracking.

While Fiona, Kay and Peter enrolled in primary school, I went to secondary grammar, despite having missed the final term of sixth grade back in Australia. Having topped my class the previous year, Mum and Dad didn't anticipate any significant problem for me in catching up.

My form mistress was Mrs Collins, a crisp, efficient woman who taught us English. Something about Mrs Collins suggested that for her a fundamental objective in life was to protect the English language from barbaric Australians. In the beginning I dreaded Mrs Collins's classes because she drew attention to my Australian accent, highlighting its shortcomings of which, until now, I had been entirely unaware. I had no appreciation of how accents varied and certainly no idea as to what constituted an Australian one. 'For heaven's sake Gordon, open your mouth when you speak,' she would implore. 'You need to pronounce your words more clearly. You can't go through life speaking like that. No one's ever going to understand. Not over here.'

'They all speak funny like that down under,' interjected one smartarse girl. Her family had migrated to Adelaide before deciding to return to England. Laughter enveloped the room although not from Mrs Collins who declined to concede anything humorous.

Outside of school, I welcomed the opportunity to explore a major metropolis for the first time and, unlike in Melbourne, Mum and Dad now considered me old enough to visit the city unsupervised and in the company of my chums. Life in and around London spawned a fascination with history which Dad nurtured carefully in the same way he tended his roses. We frequently visited museums, historical places and residences of famous writers. Occasionally we scoured the Thames mud flats in search of ancient relics. Sifting through debris, I discovered old clay pipes of which I was particularly proud. To me it was incredible that treasure of this kind was available for the taking. Refuse had been discarded in the river since time immemorial so there was unlimited booty up for grabs. Lying in bed, my treasures around me, I would dream of a tavern and the men who had once smoked my pipes.

My interest in treasure was not something new. Early on I was curious about old things and the mystery inherent in them. In part that was due to Mum who was an inveterate hoarder, worse than any of us when it came to accumulating treasure. Junk spilled out of cupboards everywhere, Mum's most prized possessions forming a shrine around the lounge-room chair into which she sank on weekday evenings. For Mum the lounge room was a place of celebration, a room oozing family history and replete with cherished memories.

However, the nature of the treasure I accumulated in England was determined to a significant extent by Dad. He introduced me to whatever he considered worthwhile and generally our interests and tastes coincided. One early passion Dad instilled was an appreciation of old books. Dad's fascination with them stemmed from a penchant for history and literature, and together we explored antique book stores, spellbound by what we encountered.

On one memorable occasion, Dad and I discovered a signed first edition copy of Charles Dickens' *Oliver Twist* displayed prominently in a dealer's front window. Dad and I were so captivated by the highly priced volume that we returned on several occasions merely to observe it. Dickens was one of the Victorian writers Dad appreciated most.

Before our departure from Melbourne, I managed to stash

away the considerable sum of thirty pounds as treasure money for our sojourn and I was committed to using it judiciously. Initial purchases included a first edition copy of *Edwin Drood*, Charles Dickens' final, unfinished novel, and a copy of the 1864 official Shakespeare folio commemorating the writer's birth 300 years previously. The Shakespeare folio was affordable only because the lithographs had been hand-coloured, decreasing the volume's value significantly.

An original page from the *Nuremberg Chronicle*, published in 1493 by Anton Koberger, the celebrated fifteenth-century European printer, was another purchase. The *Chronicle*, an encyclopaedic summary of world geography and history, contained more than eighteen hundred woodcut portraits and pictures, many used several times to illustrate objects and events varying in character and separated widely in time. No doubt readers found it disconcerting to discover fourteen portraits of kings used to represent 270 different monarchs and twenty-eight images of popes masquerading for 326 different pontiffs!

An 1821 letter written by an ancestor of Sir Alec Douglas-Home, then Conservative Party prime minister, was another item in my burgeoning collection. Written in Surrey, the letter had been despatched to Edinburgh by twopenny post, its envelope stamped with a halfpenny surcharge 'for carriage by coach with more than two wheels'. Even more special was an 1840 letter which displayed an original penny black — the world's first postage stamp — which I purchased from Stanley Gibbons in The Strand for forty-five shillings.

Another treasure was a Roman coin: a silver quinarius nearly two thousand years old, struck by a legate in Spain who completed construction of the city of Augusta Emerita, now Merida, in the province of Badajoz, destined for veterans of the V and VIII Legions whose service had expired. I obtained the coin at the

Roman baths in the city of Bath along with a leaf of pure gold, believed to be genuine, though sold without warranty, from a Roman victory crown. A wreath of bay leaves formed part of the triumphal insignia which Rome conferred upon victorious generals. In the Emperor's case, the wreath was pure gold and worn as a crown on state occasions.

One day Dad suggested we visit St Albans, a neighbouring municipality we were yet to explore. In addition to the nave of its cathedral, reputedly the world's longest, St Albans was famous for the ruins of the ancient Roman city of Verulamium which had been founded nearby across the River Ver. Before the Roman conquest Verulamium was the capital of Tasciovanus, prince of the Catuvellauni, and was later sacked by Boadicea before once again being rebuilt.

Arriving at the ruins, we encountered an archaeological team excavating a site which had produced skeletons interred with pottery and other domestic and personal artefacts. Wandering over, Dad struck up a conversation with the archaeologist supervising the dig while I stared rivetted to the treasure displayed below. When Dad explained my interest in history, I was invited to return to dig with the team should I so desire. Instantly accepting the offer, from then on every Saturday I headed for Veralamium by double-decker bus, the shards of pottery the team permitted me to keep forming an integral part of the treasure I accumulated for our eventual journey home.

Somewhere along the line, the school sportsmaster awarded me the nickname of Kanga. A likeable individual who rubbished Australia good-naturedly, Barney took an obvious shine to me. When one day he asked whether or not I played soccer, automatically I replied affirmatively, assuming that was what Australian Rules Football must be called in England. After all, Aussie Rules was the only form of football in the world —

everyone knew that. Arriving at practice, my heart sank as I realised I had claimed to play a game I had never laid eyes on before. Placed midfield, I bluffed my way along by mimicking others. Somehow I survived, in time cracking a class team.

It was around this time that another nickname surfaced unexpectedly. One day one of my classmates mentioned that he had seen a television program about Australian Aboriginals the previous evening. 'Are you Aboriginal, Gordon,' he enquired out of the blue. 'I was thinking about it after the program. They say the only coloured people in Australia are Aboriginals and you're not completely white are you? Where do your Mum and Dad come from? What nationality are they?'

Embarrassed, I blushed the way I did in Melbourne when anyone mentioned my colour or referred to me as 'Abo'. How could I respond? This wasn't something I'd expected to surface on the other side of the world. 'My parents are white but I'm adopted,' I replied eventually.

'Are you sure you haven't got any Aboriginal in you, even a tiny bit?' my classmate persisted. As others joined in discussion mounted, a consensus emerging that I must have at least some 'Abo' blood.

'Why don't we call him "Abo"?' suggested another mate jokingly. 'That's what we'll call him. You're not Kanga anymore. It's "Abo" from now on. "Abo's" shorter.'

Thus I acquired a name which embarrassed me to the depths of my soul. While all my life references to my colour had arisen, this was different, the first time I had been confronted with my race in a more formal way and at an older, more impressionable age. Discussed openly by my peers, now at twelve years of age my colour had managed to infiltrate day-to-day life in another country. When eventually we returned to Australia, a keepsake I retained was an autograph book containing affectionate farewells inscribed to 'Dear Abo'.

During our journey home, which took us by Cunard liner across the Atlantic from England to Canada, then by Greyhound bus across the United States and onwards by liner to Australia via Honolulu, Suva and Auckland, I contemplated my colour, this distinctive companion which had accompanied me as far back as my memory extended and whose presence grew stronger with each passing year. I also reflected on the incongruity of my race in relation to every other individual I knew. Whatever the truth of my story, it differed from everyone else around me. I stood out as different.

Now on the brink of my teens, my classmates in England had provided my colour with a label: Aboriginal. For the first time it had been defined specifically by my peers as a group. To a young boy of my age and circumstances, the classification was enormously confusing, despite having been questioned about my colour and referred to as 'Abo' back home in Australia. Somehow that had been different. I'd been younger and it had been easier to ignore and therefore hadn't mattered so much. But having acquired a new name used routinely, what I'd experienced in England was more organised and meaningful. It forced me to wonder seriously. What was my race? What were my origins? Was I really Aboriginal? Up until now I had thought only in terms of my colour. Never specifically in terms of race. It had always been colour which had distinguished me and placed me apart, not a particular connection with any individual race. In any case, what did I know about Aboriginals? How familiar was anyone of my age and social background with that particular subject? Back in Australia Dad had shown me material on Aboriginals that'd been in the house for years and which I glanced at periodically. From this I had learnt that traditional Aboriginals were hunters and gatherers, plus a few snippets about Aboriginal society prior to European settlement. There was also the Aboriginal axehead in Dad's study which I handled curiously from time to time and the Aboriginal middens we had explored along the coast. Whatever this amounted to, it represented the extent of my knowledge.

Enigmatic and exotic, my colour was a strange thing to contemplate, spurring confusion beyond my control. At the same time, the mystery surrounding my background was unquestionably exciting. It permitted fantasies about imagined people and places. The fantasies were private, indefinable affairs. Logical and satisfying corollaries of my sense of self, they assuaged gaps, albeit in a make-believe, superficial kind of way. However, fantasies were all that was available because in terms of definitive background, there was precious little to grasp onto in any tangible sense. In contrast with those around me, my life had been defined as different right from the outset.

For the first time it occurred to me that colour had overtaken the fact of my adoption as my paramount distinguishing feature. It had evolved quite naturally that I now viewed myself as 'coloured' rather than white. I contemplated the source of my colour which I knew didn't originate with my natural mother. Although Mum hadn't mentioned much about her, she had told me that she had met her at the Queen Vic during the week preceding my birth and that she was white and Anglo-Saxon, which suggested my colour derived from my father. That was what I had always suspected intuitively. I sensed that my natural father held the key to my 'real' identity.

I found myself wondering if he might be Aboriginal. As Pop Brodrick had suggested, that seemed the most likely possibility. Apart from its indigenous population, Australia remained overwhelmingly white despite some post-war immigration and the

Colombo Plan which, in the early fifties, opened the country for the first time this century to Asians in significant numbers, albeit on a restricted and temporary basis. For me colour equated exclusively with Aboriginals. Torres Strait Islanders and Pacific islanders descended from sugar slaves blackbirded to work on the Queensland plantations last century hadn't yet penetrated the southern urban white consciousness.

When it came to those around me, my background attracted increasing conjecture. Clearly I wasn't Anglo-Saxon and people found the fact that I didn't know my racial background intriguing, frequently observing me intently and then attempting to guess. All manner of possibilities were suggested: Greek, Italian, Spanish, Pacific Islander, Indian, Jewish, Arab, Aboriginal and others. The questioning was as normal to me as breathing. There had never been a time when it hadn't occurred; not as far back as my memory extended. I had always stood out. Greeks occasionally spoke Greek to me in the street. Italians would break out in Italian. Responding to their enquiries about my background was difficult and embarrassing because it meant I had to mention that I was adopted and didn't know my racial background precisely. I never encountered anyone else who had to do that. I mean, who didn't know their racial origins for heaven's sake? Decades later I still hadn't encountered anyone. Even Fiona, Kay and Peter who didn't know their backgrounds definitively had no reason to assume they were not Anglo-Saxons. They blended in naturally with their environment. Race wasn't an issue, at least not in the same way it was for me. My circumstances were unique.

CHAPTER 9

Scotch College

We are Scotch Collegians all
And we rally at the call
As our fathers and our brothers used to do;
For we dearly love the name,
And will ever guard the fame
Of the School that wears the cardinal, gold and blue.

Chorus
'Good old Scotch!' we'll shout in chorus,
As our hearts with ardour glow.
There's no other school, we swear,
That can with 'The Scotch' compare;
We have searched the whole world over, and we know.

First verse and chorus of the 'College Song'

Three days after arriving in Sydney on the *Arcadia*, our world trip concluded, I found myself at morning assembly on the first day of third term at Scotch College, the old and distinguished

Melbourne boys' private school whose earliest stated goal was 'to provide superior education to young men'. Knowing only two boys from primary school out of the twelve hundred students present, and feeling disoriented and alone, I struggled not to cry.

It was my turn to continue a hallowed Brodrick family tradition. Pop Brodrick had relished his time at Scotch, as had Mum's brother Warren. And as far back as I could remember I learnt to feel proud that Warren's name was inscribed on the school's honour board, where those who had sacrificed their lives in the two world wars were remembered. However, Scotch College and I were incompatible from the outset.

To get ahead at this elite institution where we were constantly reminded how privileged we were, one needed to excel, either academically or at sport, and I excelled at neither. Not because I lacked ability but rather because I felt chronically unsettled and detached, as if I didn't belong. In retrospect, this was a consequence of our trip. Despite the excitement of seeing friends again and reliving the familiar anew, I felt despondent and uninterested in my surroundings. I wasn't settling down. Our year overseas had been a defining experience, one which had broadened my horizons, altering irrevocably my perception of the world and of my own particular place within it. Now I found the process of re-establishing myself in Melbourne and becoming accustomed to a new and authoritarian school overwhelmingly difficult. And so, with profound regret, the previous year was relegated to the past. It would be years before I would ever make serious mention of our trip to a single schoolmate.

Starting in third term meant I was behind my classmates academically, a disadvantage exacerbated by differences in the Scotch and East Barnet curricula. Nor was my form master, memorable for his penchant for slicing the backsides of students with a ruler while they touched their toes, a source of inspiration.

I resented the fact that undertaking sport twice weekly was compulsory, and that detentions were awarded for misdemeanours such as being caught outside the school in uniform without one's middle suit coat button done up or minus the school cap. School prefects were entitled to make students write out lines and the school captain could, with the principal's consent, cane students, although that punishment generally remained the personal domain of Mr Healey, the principal, who was a strict disciplinarian.

However, what I really detested was military cadets which, along with most of my peers, I joined in third form when all boys were required to participate either in cadets, scouts or social services. The Scotch College cadet corps was the largest school cadet corps in Australia and the college was inordinately proud of this. The cadets rated highest in status at the school and was what you were really expected to select, although scouts also attracted approval, albeit to a lesser extent. The real anathema was social services, reserved in the school culture for bludgers. No one keen to progress within the school system selected that particular option, lamentable from my point of view because it appealed strongly. While others pursued cadets or scouts, social service mavericks spent Thursday afternoons helping at the local blind institute or at a nearby centre for handicapped children. Besides providing a valuable community service, social services was meant to teach boys the importance of tolerance, understanding, patience and respect.

Pressured by this intimidating hierarchy, I ignored my instincts and opted for cadets, eventually taking up the tuba in order to join the military band. Learning to play the tuba was undoubtedly one of the most boring activities I ever pursued. However, it did provide an escape from more military-type activities, although unfortunately not the annual cadet camp at Puckapunyal where we sacrificed one full week of our treasured second-term vacations.

Like a number of my peers, I detested cadet camp, particularly on frosty winter mornings when band members arose before dawn to play reveille to waken the 'troops'. Some mornings it was so cold my lips stuck to the instrument's mouthpiece until freed by saliva. And although firing 303s, orientation courses and bivouacs were certainly the stuff of Boy's Own Annuals, I preferred time spent doing things that really interested me or in the company of friends outside school. By the time sixth form arrrived, the lure of social services proved irresistable. Advising Mr Healey of my desire to swap services, I was lectured sternly on the merits of cadets before being informed that my request would in fact be granted on condition that I write a letter seeking permission to make the change. Handing the letter over, the principal criticised a point of grammar and requested an amended version before approval was formally conferred.

For me, however, the defining feature of Scotch had nothing to do with academic pursuits, sport, cadets, or other aspects of school life. Scotch influenced me in a far more fundamental and enduring manner, the importance of which I only grasped fully much later. More than any other influence which shaped me during adolescence, Scotch played a crucial role in fostering my sense of racial difference, of not being Anglo-Saxon, of possessing a dimension to my being that was increasingly responsible for confusion and enquiry. It was at Scotch that I learnt about racism and inequality.

References to my colour and questions about my race surfaced from the very beginning. That was something I had anticipated. After all, colour and race were already intrinsic features of life. But in contrast with my primary school years and East Barnet, the tone was unmistakably different. In England, 'Abo' had been uttered affectionately, as a term of endearment. This was not the case at Scotch.

When someone called me 'Abo' during my initial years, on the few occasions that it occurred, I was able to turn a blind eye. By convincing myself that it was inoffensive and not worth dwelling upon, I managed to cope. By third form, however, the nature of the antagonism and my response to it had altered dramatically.

I don't remember precisely how it began, but encouraged by a ringleader, as teenage boys so frequently are, a number of boys decided that calling me 'Abo' could provide entertainment. Soon I found that whenever I appeared during recess or at lunchtime, I would find myself subjected to a chant of 'Abo' which sometimes reverberated around the entire senior school quadrangle, situated at the heart of the college. Within a short space of time, 'Abo' was alternated with 'Boong' — scarcely an improvement. There was nothing affectionate or well meaning in the way those words were spat, although they never appeared to imply a threat of violence.

Soon the name calling dominated my perception of the school entirely. In time I came to dread attending. The journey to school involved two tram rides. On weekday mornings, I would wait apprehensively for the tram's arrival, hopeful that none of my detractors would be on board. Timing was of the essence. Their absence bestowed an unhassled journey to school. Boarding the tram, I would glance around uneasily to ascertain whether or not I was safe. Often I was not. The ringleader, who travelled on the same route, would be on the lookout for me to board, primed to initiate the chant of 'Abo' which, escalating embarrassingly as others joined in, swelled into an anthem of intimidating proportions, while other passengers turned away.

To a boy in his early teens, humiliation of this kind made school unbearable. It was impossible to avoid the ceaseless taunting. Neither defence nor escape were possible. Arriving home, I would retreat to my bedroom, thankful at least that Mum and Dad had no idea of what was taking place. I would have died with embarrassment had they ever heard anyone say any of this to me, although of course my parents had overheard comments already and did so increasingly as the years passed. In these moments of anguish and depression, I pondered my racial background and its significant gaps.

I thought again about what Mum had told me about my disrupted background. Since our return from England she had explained further, informing me that my mother had been a Sydneysider named Colette and that like many other single, pregnant women she had travelled interstate to hide her pregnancy and have her baby on the quiet. I recalled vividly how on one occasion when Mum was upset with me she had referred to Colette and how disappointed she would be were she able to witness my behaviour. Mum's comment had really stung. Confrontingly, it had conjured up this crucial yet invisible player at the heart of my own compelling mystery; a woman about whom I had fantasised ever since being old enough to understand the meaning of adoption. I imagined how she might look and who and where she might be. Unexpectedly, sometimes Colette entered my psyche, although this felt entirely natural. I understood that if you were adopted some parts of you remained invisible but existed nonetheless. Colette fell naturally into this category, drifting in and out of my consciousness.

I began thinking of this woman as someone real, a tangible person. I found it both startling and disturbing to acknowledge she actually existed. The realisation jolted my being. Mum had already described Colette's physical appearance or at least the defining characteristics of her face. That information had fascinated me for years, although visualising her proved impossible no matter how hard I tried.

I also tried to imagine how Colette must have felt on the day of my birth, 21 June 1952; a depressing winter's day on which, due to inclement weather, Victoria found itself without a race meeting of any kind, unprecedented for a Saturday. That same day, Melbourne professional strongman Young Apollo, who achieved notoriety for stunts which included having cars run over him while lying on a bed of spikes and hauling a fully loaded tram or a semi-trailer loaded with two elephants by his teeth, was discovered in a room in North Carlton with a bullet wound below the heart.

Curiously, that day the Melbourne *Herald* also reported that in Argentina, where a quarter of a century later I would spend four years as a diplomat, allegations circulated that dictator Juan Peron had used secret torture chambers for the punishment of political enemies. The day after my birth, special masses were conducted in every Argentine Catholic church for Eva Peron, ravaged by the cancer that would claim her later that year.

When it came to my natural father, Mum knew nothing whatsoever other than what she had gleaned from Auntie Rose. Based on her discussions with Colette, Rose claimed he had been an Agricultural Science student at Sydney University, although she wasn't entirely sure. And despite the absence of conclusive proof, Auntie Rose insisted he was white. In later years when my racial background attracted increasing speculation, Rose could never accept the notion that my natural father might be coloured or Aboriginal, although she would revise her opinion eventually, conceding that perhaps he had arrived in Australia under the Colombo Plan.

I thought further about race and colour in relation to my father. I sensed in my heart that my father wasn't white but lacked conclusive proof to the contrary. Other than a handful of Chinese boys at school, I knew no one whose parents were not Anglo-Saxon or white. There were no relevant role models. My father's colour, and my unwavering commitment to its as yet unestablished authenticity, were guarded fiercely by me among life's fundamental, unchallengeable truths. I had no idea where he might have come from but, wherever it was, people there weren't white. Never could anyone have convinced me otherwise.

Not for the first time since returning from abroad, I found myself wondering again about whether or not he might be Aboriginal. When I considered it, Aboriginality did provide a logical explanation. As I had concluded when younger, most coloured people in Australia were Aboriginal and now I found myself surrounded by others who suggested I was too. What didn't add up however was Auntie Rose's understanding that my father had attended university. While I had no idea how many Aboriginals undertook university studies in Australia, I recognised the numbers would be few. Still, there was no proof that Auntie Rose's information was accurate, and I held an unflinching belief in my father's colour; instinct and experience convinced me of that. My mind returned to Scotch and how unhappy I had become. Was it any wonder that I never studied or participated in school activities committedly? Why were my energies consumed with confused identity and race? I decided that if the taunting continued, I would refuse to return to school.

On several occasions I spoke confidentially to the ringleader and one or two acolytes requesting that they desist. My pleas only encouraged them further. Desperately unhappy, I forwarded an 'anonymous' letter to Mr Healey realising of course that the letter would be anything but anonymous. Its writer would be apparent immediately. It could only have come from me. There was no other mixed-blood boy to have written it. All that was incidental. What I was planning would be effective and that was what mattered.

After mailing the letter, which explained that a third-form boy was being taunted because of his colour and requested the headmaster's intervention to assist, I waited uneasily for something to happen. I didn't have to wait long. Two days later I was called out of class and advised that the principal wished to see me.

Entering the office, I encountered Mr Healey seated calmly behind his desk. 'Sit down Gordon,' he requested, directing me towards an empty chair. I was taken aback at being addressed by my Christian name. I had never heard the principal do that. We were always referred to by our surnames.

'Why did you write this,' enquired Mr Healey, passing my letter back over.

I glanced around uncomfortably. 'Because I couldn't stand the ribbing anymore,' I murmured softly.

'Has this been going on for long?' he continued sympathetically.

'Yes,' I responded, before offering a detailed explanation of precisely what had been occurring.

'I really don't know what to say,' replied Mr Healey when I concluded. 'I find this type of behaviour reprehensible. I refuse to tolerate it within the school. Please accept my apologies. I really am sorry. I'm not sure what else I can add. Now I'd like you to tell me precisely who was involved. I'll require all the names.'

'If you don't mind sir, I'd prefer not to provide those,' I responded. 'Everyone'll think I'm a dobber. Please sir, I can't do that.'

Mr Healey digested my words before responding. 'All right Gordon, on this occasion I'll respect your wishes but you must provide the name of the ringleader. I'll definitely be speaking to that particular boy. Don't worry, this will be dealt with discreetly. You'll suffer no further distress.' I gave him the name.

Leaving the principal's office, I contemplated Mr Healey's unanticipated sensitivity. The principal who terrified everyone had revealed a gentler, more human side; one which I had observed only from afar whenever he spoke with his sons, both students at the school. I always gained the impression that the Healey boys were uncomfortable with the fact that their father was principal and with the ambiguous position that placed them in with their peers.

That same day the taunting ceased entirely and although we never discussed the situation directly, I realised from the embarrassed and sheepish look upon his face that the ringleader had been soundly reprimanded by the headmaster. Given that no one else said anything, I assumed that he had been instructed to ensure that others stopped taunting me too. Years later, I encountered a Scotch boy who was big enough to refer to and apologise for the treatment which had been inflicted.

In 1993, following Colin Healey's death, I recalled words written by distinguished old boy Sir Archibald Glenn following the principal's retirement in 1975. 'He has put duty to the school first and foremost. He has never courted popularity to the detriment of discipline, but behind the fiery appearance is essentially a shy, sensitive man. Many a boy has said, "You really get to know Mr Healey when you find yourself in trouble".' While I still disliked what he represented, three decades later, recalling how sensitively Colin Healey had managed my problem, I found myself unwilling to disagree with Glenn's words.

CHAPTER 10

Adolescence

Within a couple of years of returning to Australia I had become active sexually, losing my virginity long before most of my peers, in circumstances which even now I prefer not to describe. However, more regular dalliances with the opposite sex occurred only infrequently until fourth form when at dancing class we were introduced to girls a year below us from neighbouring private schools. This was our first opportunity to interact socially with the other gender on a sanctioned and ongoing basis.

Dancing class was conducted by Hans Meyer and his wife, a baroness with a Hapsburg connection which I never entirely understood. Mr Meyer, an expatriate Austrian, also Venezuela's honorary-consul, was a monocled, distinguished looking gentleman; his wife was memorable for her stiffly lacquered bouffant hair, her impeccable dress, and the pervasive waft of perfume which accompanied her whenever she entered the room. The Meyers' objective was to teach us how to interact socially and how to dance. However, no one who attended was there for either of these purposes. Rather, we were preoccupied with the rituals of adolescent mating.

The first half of dancing class consisted of tuition in more formal dances, including the foxtrot and waltz, about which none of us understood a thing and in which nobody was remotely interested. This initial segment of the evening bore no relevance to our lives whatsoever. 'Not like that,' the Baroness would shriek despairingly in heavily accented English. We boys lived in fear of being accosted by her and swirled embarrassingly around the room, clutching the Baroness's rigidly corseted waist in unrestricted view of all our mates. Some dances involved multiple partners, the plump girls invariably squeezing you more tightly.

The latter part of the evening, awaited desperately by everyone, enabled you to dance with the partner of your choice to contemporary hits by bands such as The Strangers — the resident band on the popular television 'Go Show' who once played at the annual school dance — The Loved Ones, The Mamas and the Papas (who everyone was into), The Beatles, and even The Rolling Stones. Most boys, myself included, attended in their regular grey school uniform, sporting the grooviest tie they could lay their hands on. The tie was crucial, providing the one opportunity to distinguish oneself and assert individuality. With a tinge of jealousy, we would observe the handful of boys privileged to possess another suit and the air of confident superiority they exuded. However, the coolest boys were those who chose not to attend at all, loitering outside instead in clusters, cigarettes between lips, awaiting whatever social opportunity might present itself for later in the evening.

Integral to our inchoate socialising with the opposite sex and intrinsic to the social agenda were parties, the receipt or not of an invitation constituting an indication of your worth and popularity.

Usually I scored decently because I was relatively popular. Invitations to these events were greatly anticipated, especially for the opportunities the parties provided to devour flasks of spirits smuggled inside for rapid inebriation before parents retreated, lights were lowered and couples retired to dim corners.

While more experienced sexually than the majority of my contemporaries, or so I imagined, sex had already acquired an even greater illicit dimension because, around the same time as dancing class, I had guiltily experimented sexually with a classmate who had propositioned me on an otherwise unexceptional day. Although I had no idea what our activity amounted to, I understood its unacceptability in the overall scheme of things, even though personally I didn't see a problem and repeated it, as much as a gesture of protest as anything else. Like the rest of my generation I had been indoctrinated with the belief that anything to do with homosexuality was perverse and abnormal. Nothing was remotely as unconscionable as that, although at least, unlike the Catholic miscreants at a nearby college, I knew I wasn't destined for hell. In any case, not once having smoked a cigarette surreptitiously with the serious school rebels, I knew I wasn't bad.

During this phase of adolescence I found myself consumed by a rebelliousness and dissatisfaction that was difficult to explain. I argued frequently with Mum and Dad, avoided homework, plagiarising instead the efforts of others, spent excessive time outside the home, abused my lungs with cigarettes, and snuck out at night to visit city venues where purple hearts and other amphetamines were available. In short, I was undermining Mum and Dad's clearly defined ideas of what I might usefully be doing. Repeated exhortations that I would suffer academically were inconsequential to a dissatisfied teenager on the brink of sixteen with no concept of what might lie ahead. A change of school was suggested from time to time but nothing ever eventuated. Scotch was my second school in four years and despite my restlessness I had no desire to embark on a third. Instead, I simply accepted Scotch as an intractable element of life, conscious it would eventually end.

The heady confusion of adolescence was intensified by the distraction of my identity. Although the racial taunting had ceased, I often wondered about that other individual I had been at birth with a name and background different from the one I now possessed. Colette had named me Paul, and even though in a formal sense Paul had ceased to exist, my spirit possessed a strong sense of that other person. I knew there were elements of him essential to me and that he survived, albeit incompletely, by virtue of my existence; this individual who in other circumstances I might have become. It was a curious thing.

I also dwelt upon myself in relation to my siblings. We shared a multitude of attributes, having been raised together by the same parents. However, I found myself increasingly aware that even that degree of shared experience failed to infiltrate the essence of each of us as individuals. Peter was practical with no interest in anything much which appealed to me. He enjoyed mathematics and was gifted with his hands. During fifth form, Peter jettisoned Scotch in favour of a technical college, his practical bent leading him eventually to establish a successful motor mechanics business. By comparison, I was clumsy at manual tasks.

Yet for all the dissimilarities of tastes and lifestyles, I valued my relationship with my brother intensely. Without reservation we viewed each other as brothers with strong and genuine respect for one another. And we were always available to each other in moments of crisis.

My relationships with my two sisters differed again. While similar in age, Fiona and I shared few interests and didn't spend much time together. It was an uneasy relationship and we sparred regularly. I never understood precisely why that was, although perhaps the proximity of our ages was responsible and at times I must have been a difficult and overbearing brother, especially when younger. My relationship with Kay was slightly more substantial, although at this stage there was no indication of the close friendship that my younger sister and I would share later on. Kay was several years my junior and therefore outside my social milieu.

At the same time that I contemplated my adoptive siblings and where Gordon Matthews belonged in the universe, I found myself wondering whether or not I might possess natural brothers and sisters and, if so, what they might be like and how much we might have in common. For some reason I had always assumed that my natural parents married following my birth and that I possessed other brothers and sisters. On what basis I concluded this I have no idea given that a different scenario seemed far more likely. Few single women subsequently married the fathers of their relinquished babies. Nevertheless, I felt confident that somewhere out there I possessed another family.

Apart from the rampant turmoil which characterised my behaviour so markedly, at least some stability was evident in my adolescence. During the latter years of secondary school, part of my social life revolved around the local Presbyterian church youth group and, for a time, I served as president. Sunday school had been introduced at an early age and our weekly attendance was something which I enjoyed, although primarily for the social opportunities which it provided rather than for anything remotely spiritual or religious. However, my Christian credentials had surged to the fore on several occasions during childhood, including when at eight years of age I flawlessly recited the Ten Commandments in front of the entire Sunday school, Dad rewarding me with a leather bound copy of the *Psalms of David*, my initials inscribed boldly in gold.

Also, in the company of other Presbyterian Fellowship Association members, I sometimes visited a local children's home called The Gables where we spent Saturday afternoons with the children. Residents included orphans, wards of the state, children awaiting placement in foster homes, intellectually challenged children and a five-year-old Aboriginal boy whom I attracted like a magnet. Like mine, Neville Austin's background was unclear. I never knew what had happened to his parents or if he had been forcibly removed from his family by white welfare like many other Aboriginal children.

In a very short space of time I became the focus of Neville's affection. Every Saturday he would wait astride The Gables fence as I strolled up the hill in the company of other group members. From the moment I arrived, I found my time monopolised by my new companion who refused to let me out of his sight. Soon I felt increasingly responsible for Neville's welfare, visiting also on several afternoons during the week. As always, Neville would wait expectantly for my arrival clutching the rope handle of the go-kart he treasured — the only present he had ever received, knocked up from old wooden crates by a handyman at the home. In time, he started coming home and Mum and I found ourselves discussing his future. Mum became so fond of him that she even considered fostering him. While Mum gave the idea serious thought, for some reason it didn't progress and I never pursued it.

Visiting The Gables not long after, I discovered that Neville had been fostered by a family in the western suburbs and was no longer there. After obtaining their number, I phoned to introduce myself, enquire about my friend's well-being and establish if I could visit. Agreeing to a meeting the following weekend, Neville's new foster mother appeared delighted that I had called. However, not long before the scheduled visit, she phoned to explain that on mentioning me Neville had become upset. In view of that, she and her husband considered it might be preferable if I didn't visit and contact ceased.

I contemplated my brief, intense relationship with Neville and what had drawn us together. What had inspired my interest in someone so much younger? I realised that, partially at least, it had been because Neville was Aboriginal. Although on several occasions in my early teens I had encountered Aboriginals in the city who had stared and nodded in recognition, I remained a curious teenager who had never encountered an indigenous Australian but who found himself increasingly preoccupied with his own racial background, believing more and more each day that he might be Aboriginal.

In addition to this encounter with Neville and the effect it had upon me, the only other specific event which caused me to contemplate indigenous Australians during those final years at Scotch was uncharacteristically academic; matriculation Australian History. Although Aboriginals had always been neglected by historians — the fringe dwellers of Australian historiography as one academic would describe them not much later — the annual matriculation examination offered a token essay question on Aboriginals, invariably of a pre-history nature, tackled by only a handful of teachers and students throughout the state.

However, I had read Professor D.J. Mulvaney's *Pre-history of Australia* published earlier that year and one of only a handful of comprehensive texts available which dealt with Aboriginals in any illuminating or meaningful way. Just one year prior to my matriculation, Professor Stanner, the noted Australian anthropologist who worked determinedly to encourage a more positive approach towards indigenous Australians, referred to 'the great Australian silence' prevailing in the wider community and the 'emptiness of conscience and compassion' in relation to Aboriginal Australians. Still, the absence of concern with Aboriginals and lack of any positive approach to their culture and their consequential stereotyping was scarcely surprising given that until the early 1960s the *Bulletin* had heralded proudly in its masthead 'Australia for the white man'.

When the last day of school finally arrived, along with other sixth-form students I returned for final assembly following a two-week absence to prepare for our matriculation exams. An hour or so before assembly commenced, I found myself taken aside by a teacher I disliked intensely.

'Matthews. Why's your hair touching your ears?' he enquired, direct and abrasive. Our hair wasn't permitted to touch ears or shirt collars.

'You've never been the warm, engaging kind, have you?' I ruminated privately, suppressing the contempt which his comment provoked. I wondered why he hadn't singled out anyone else. After two weeks' absence at the end of the school year, I was hardly the only offender. 'Sir, it's only just touching,' I replied. 'Surely that's not serious.'

'Go and have it cut now,' he replied curtly. 'And make sure you come back.' Suppressing anger, reluctantly I agreed.

I contemplated my situation. I was at Scotch for the very last time. I had fantasised about this moment more times than I could possibly remember. An exhilarating sense of liberation overwhelmed me. The fact that soon I would be free spun tantalisingly around my head. Walking towards the school gates, through the serene and exquisite grounds which had always struck me as incongruous given my perceptions of the school, I realised I would not be returning for final assembly. Scotch College had not been a happy experience. There was no need for a formal farewell.

The realisation that I wasn't returning to link arms and sing 'Auld Lang Syne', with other school leavers propelled me. Soon I ran faster and faster, on towards the gates, then ecstatically out into the world. Finally I was free.

CHAPTER 11

Tasmania

One Friday night, I dropped in at a pub where a group of mates met sometimes for a drink and word of a party. By chance, I encountered an acquaintance I hadn't seen for ages. Like the rest of us, Mike Stuart had just completed secondary school, although without obtaining any honours, which meant it remained unclear if he would be accepted for university studies in Victoria. Consequently, Mike was looking for a university interstate with less rigorous entry requirements.

'Do you know what I've decided to do?' my friend asked me. 'I'm going to check out the University of Tasmania in Hobart. Tassie's a great spot. We used to visit there for Christmas holidays. I've heard the standard's as high as over here but that there's fewer students. They say it's easier to get in.'

Although I remained silent, there and then I decided to tag along. Like Mike, I was interested only in an arts degree although neither of us had the faintest idea what we would do once we graduated. But we could worry about that later.

Mike made everything sound incredibly straightforward. With

the student discount the airlines offered, the return fare to Tasmania was insignificant. Once there, Mike had family friends to stay with in the Derwent Valley outside Hobart which meant expenses would be minimal. I'd never been to Tasmania, aware only of what mainlanders know: Truganini, Port Arthur, and the wilderness.

Unlike Mike, I wasn't obliged to leave Melbourne to find a tertiary institution that would accept me. Nevertheless, the thought of escaping for a few years appealed considerably and, while never having considered Tasmania, my instincts encouraged me to give it a go. 'If nothing else, I'll at least get to experience another state. If things don't work out, I'll just study here in Melbourne,' I decided.

Next morning I sprang out of bed to confront Mum and Dad with my plan. There wasn't much time to get organised. Mike was taking an early afternoon flight and there were many things to do before then, assuming Mum and Dad would come through with the cash. Although well broken in to my spur-of-the-moment whims, Mum and Dad were somewhat bemused by my unexpected interest in Tasmania but agreed to help.

We stayed only a couple of days, too short for anything other than a superficial look, but Hobart's picture postcard setting instantly attracted me. Nestled below Mt Wellington on the Derwent River estuary, the city reminded me of a miniature version of Sydney. When an offer from the university arrived a few weeks later I had effectively made up my mind. Ironically, poor Mike failed to get in.

Late in February, a week or so before classes began, I returned to Hobart to enrol and find somewhere to live. Suddenly life was changing dramatically. Now for the first time I was on my own. Not knowing a soul in Hobart, apart from some distant relatives with whom I stayed briefly when I first arrived, I decided to board with a family to ease the transition. Soon I found myself living in the suburb of Mount Stuart which provided a spectacular panorama of the river and surrounding harbour.

I studied English literature, psychology, philosophy and political science. Like all first-year political science students, in addition to lectures I attended tutorials which were conducted by Dick Rutenburg, a naturalist passionately committed to the preservation of native flora and fauna and Tasmania's Aboriginal history and culture.

An active supporter of various commendable causes, Dick laboured tirelessly on behalf of Aboriginal people, involving himself closely in ABSCHOL, the scheme begun in 1961 and sponsored by the Australian Union of Students which provided scholarships to enable Aboriginal students to undertake further education. While pure-blood Aboriginals — a description offensive to indigenous Australians who think in terms of identity, never percentages of blood — had been annihilated more than a century earlier, their descendents survived, albeit in modest numbers. Like Aboriginals elsewhere in the country, those who acknowledged their Aboriginal heritage were entitled to receive Commonwealth study grants which provided financial support to undertake mainstream education. The scheme had been introduced to address the gaping disparity between white and black educational achievement.

A staunch advocate of Aboriginal education, Dick tracked down individuals who qualified for grants to inform them of their entitlements. Many of those he approached were completely unaware of the scheme's existence and sometimes of their own Aboriginality.

Towards the end of my first year, Dick sidled up unexpectedly in the university cafeteria. While we had spoken briefly during classes, Dick and I had never engaged in a serious conversation.

'Do you mind if we talk for a few minutes Gordon? Let me buy you a coffee,' ventured Dick. A moment later, I found myself seated opposite him wondering what on earth he might wish to discuss.

'I hope you don't mind me asking you this mate, but I've been wanting to know whether you're of Aboriginal descent? I've been curious ever since I first laid eyes on you. Your physical appearance makes me wonder. What's your racial background?'

I could hardly believe what I was hearing. I was unprepared for Dick's directness.

'Well, I could be Aboriginal,' I replied hesitantly. 'It's certainly occurred to me before. However, I don't know my racial background precisely. I'm adopted. I've never fully explored my origins and no one appears to know the truth conclusively. There's no firm proof in relation to anything although my mother also believes I could be Aboriginal. Heaps of people have suggested that over the years.'

Dick observed me intently. 'And what do you think? What's your opinion? That's the important thing. Don't your instincts tell you that you're probably Koori? After all, there's probably not too many alternatives. A helluva lot of people of Aboriginal descent were adopted out, some without even knowing they possessed Aboriginal blood. That fact was ignored due to the government's assimilation policies. No one considered it important. It was assumed that Aboriginals would eventually just die out. You know, blend into white Australia and vanish. There are thousands of people out there of Aboriginal descent who don't even know it. I reckon you could be one of them.'

Lighting a cigarette, I drew back heavily. The intimacy of the conversation was becoming uncomfortable.

Dick delved further. 'Have you ever thought about trying to find out about your background? Tell me about your adoption.

How was it arranged? There must be someone you can ask?' I explained to Dick how Mum had been a doctor at the Queen Vic and how Auntie Rose had arranged my adoption.

'Wouldn't you like to discover the truth about your racial background?' he suggested. 'Surely you're curious. If I was in your situation I'd be dying to know. Then again, everyone's different I guess. Perhaps it doesn't matter to you. Anyhow, have a think about what I've said. If you want to investigate your racial background I'd be prepared to help. I could make some preliminary enquiries on your behalf by phoning your Auntie Rose to see what information she can provide. From the sound of it, she probably knows more than anyone else.'

That conversation with Dick left me deeply disturbed. The idea of establishing my racial background excited me and had irresistible appeal. For the first time in my life, a complete identity was on offer — and from a total stranger.

On the other hand, part of me still relished the uncertainty surrounding my race. I thought again about how not knowing conclusively had always made me feel special as far back as I could remember. But now the offer of an identity swam tantalisingly around my head. How many people in my place would choose to knock back an opportunity such as this? Instantly I realised that I wasn't one.

Dick and I spoke again a few days later. 'Well, have you decided what you want to do?' he enquired. 'Do you want me to phone her or not?' Apprehensive about what Mum and Dad might think, I wavered, conscious at the same time that nothing in the world could make me say no.

'OK. Why, don't you get on with it?' I urged. 'Go ahead and call her at the Queen Vic. I'd prefer that you call rather than me. I think I'd feel a bit uncomfortable. I should warn you though, I haven't the faintest idea what Rose will tell you. I've told you all that I'm aware she knows. I have no idea whether or not she can add anything. God knows how she'll respond when you mention what you're calling about; she's bound to get a shock and will probably react defensively. Remember, she won't have a clue who you are, she's among my mother's oldest friends and I've never raised any of this directly with her before. Anyhow, see how you go.'

Throughout the rest of the day I dwelt on Dick phoning Auntie Rose. Obviously he suspected, and I instinctively also, that I possessed Aboriginal blood. Finally someone had appeared to solve the mystery of my race.

Encountering Dick several days later, I felt a rush of adrenalin. I was surprised that Dick hadn't contacted me already. He was unexpectedly subdued. 'Well, how did it go?' I enquired. 'Have you had a chance to speak with her yet?'

For a moment Dick said nothing. 'Yes, I have,' he replied eventually. 'Unfortunately things didn't go all that well.' Disappointment permeated his voice. 'Auntie Rose doesn't think there's any way you could be Aboriginal. Mind you, she doesn't seem to possess firm proof to the contrary I hasten to add. There are gaps in her story. I don't reckon she knows anything like the complete picture. She's unclear about the racial background of your father, even though she maintains that he was white. I don't think she can tolerate the idea that you might be of Aboriginal descent.'

'But what exactly did she say?' I pressed. 'I want to know exactly what she told you.'

'Well, she confirmed what you'd already said. That your natural mother was an Anglo-Saxon woman who travelled from Sydney to Melbourne to have her baby and that your father studied at Sydney University. As far as your father's racial background goes, Rose insists that he was white. She said she couldn't imagine how you or anyone else could possibly think you were coloured which is ridiculous as far as I'm concerned. Just look at you for God's sake! You're hardly fair-skinned. In my view there's no way your father was Anglo-Saxon. Rose's just kidding herself. I only have to look at you to know what she says doesn't add up.'

Everything Dick said rang true. Auntie Rose's attitude rankled deeply. 'I don't give a damn what Auntie Rose believes,' I snapped. 'I think I'm Aboriginal. I can't explain how but I've always known intuitively that my father wasn't white. If that's true, I agree with you that it's most likely that I'm Aboriginal. Listen Dick. I want my identity. What am I going to do? You've ignited something. I'm not going to compromise on this one. I've lived without my identity for far too long.'

'Why don't you have a careful think about your situation and precisely what you want to do, if anything,' suggested Dick sympathetically. 'Now tell me again. Do you really believe you're Aboriginal? You know what my view is and my instincts don't often let me down. I reckon you must have Aboriginal blood.'

His tone grew increasingly confidential. 'You're probably not aware of this. But if you believe you're of Aboriginal descent and identify as Aboriginal, you're entitled to a Commonwealth Aboriginal study grant. If you genuinely believe you're Aboriginal and are prepared to acknowledge your background, then I'll help you as much as I possibly can. Have a think about it.

'Obviously you don't have to decide here and now,' he continued. 'However, this is what we could do. For starters I could talk to the Commonwealth education authorities on your behalf to explain your situation and establish whether or not you do in fact qualify formally. Provided you really believe you're Aboriginal, I can't see any problems. Why don't you think about it and speak to your parents when you return home for Christmas. Let me know what you want to do when you get back in the New Year. The final decision is clearly yours.'

CHAPTER 12

Establishing an Identity

Over the weeks, I thought constantly about what Dick and I had discussed. By offering me a complete identity, Dick had jangled the keys to Pandora's Box. Through absolutely no fault of my own, definite proof of my race was frustratingly absent. At the bottom line what counted for me was the fact that I believed that my father wasn't white, which from my perspective meant he had to be Aboriginal. At twenty years of age with my background, that seemed the credible scenario.

I thought about looking for Colette Darcy in order to establish the truth but realised it was out of the question. The idea was unbearably confronting, beyond the realms of possibility. I had never thought seriously about looking and besides Mum might feel violated and I knew I wasn't ready for anything like that. The idea vanished instantly.

Back in Melbourne for Christmas, I broached my interest in claiming Aboriginality with Mum and Dad separately. Mum didn't seem particularly perturbed when I explained how Dick Rutenburg had approached me and that now, following careful consideration, I wished to identify formally as Aboriginal and apply for a grant. Auntie Rose had mentioned Dick's phone call, so Mum had realised something was afoot before I raised the subject myself. We discussed everything at leisure over a cup of tea.

'This has been a problem for an awfully long time, hasn't it?' commented Mum.

'Mum you don't need to ask me that. You know everything. You've seen the hassles that not knowing has caused; what happened while I was growing up and at Scotch. Now I want to establish an identity and complete the picture once and for all. The problem is determining the truth. Crucial pieces are missing. Dick discovered that talking to Rose. She maintains my father was white but I don't know how she can say that. I don't believe it for a second. Like I told Dick, I know without a shred of doubt my father was coloured. I don't need anyone to tell me that. I've always believed it and I've noticed that with the years you have too.'

'I know you've thought for a long time that you were probably Aboriginal,' acknowledged Mum. 'And no one knows better than me how many other people have assumed the same thing. But I honestly don't know your natural father's origins. As far as I'm concerned what really matters is what you believe yourself because, as the two of us know, conclusive proof is unavailable. Deep down, do you believe you're Aboriginal? That's what really counts.'

'Yes I do Mum,' I responded. 'What other explanation is there? The only thing that doesn't add up completely is the fact that Auntie Rose says Colette told her my father was a student at Sydney University. How many Aboriginals studied at Sydney University in the early 1950s? I doubt any made it that far, although there might have been one or two. Anyhow, Auntie Rose doesn't know the full picture so who the hell can say? Maybe Colette didn't reveal the entire truth. If my natural father was in fact Aboriginal, it's likely that Colette wouldn't have mentioned anything in order to protect my interests. An Aboriginal father was hardly a plus for a child up for adoption back then.'

'Well darling,' Mum said, 'I think it's for you to follow your instincts and do what you feel is right. You're the only one who has to live with your decision, no one else. If you think you're Aboriginal and accept a grant, then you have my blessing provided you truly believe in what you're doing.'

Poor old Dad had more difficulty with the idea of an Aboriginal son than did Mum. Perhaps because of his belief that I might be a Pacific islander, although I didn't learn about that until years later. Dad was frequently baffled by whatever it was that I happened to be getting up to. As if returning from Tasmania with a pierced ear wasn't enough, now I was telling him that I wanted to be Aboriginal. I privately wondered if in Dad's mind some arcane linkage existed between an Aboriginal identity and a pierced ear. What had transpired down in Hobart was unbelievably difficult for him to grasp. However, he was unable to offer an alternative practical solution to my dilemma.

'What you do is up to you,' Dad finally pronounced. 'But remember one thing. If you decide to be Aboriginal, you'll live with that forever.'

I had no problem with that. Now that my mind was made up, I wasn't concerned about the future. From my perspective I had considered everything.

'I know that Dad,' I replied irritably. 'How stupid do you think I am? I've decided what I want to do. No one's ever thought I'm Anglo-Saxon. Now I'm going to be Aboriginal; I've certainly earned the right to be and, most importantly, I believe that I am. I wouldn't do this otherwise. When I get back to Hobart I'm going to contact Dick Rutenburg and apply for a grant. A grant confers an identity. From now on I'm Aboriginal.' Dad listened silently.

While proclaiming my Aboriginality, I also recognised that my conclusion was not the one that everyone would have reached. Certainly a leap of faith was involved, but I found the logic compelling and, after carefully examining my motives and concluding they were pure, decided to follow my instincts.

I was excited by my new status. For the first time I felt a completeness impossible to explain. Now I could actually say who and what I was. My ruptured identity had been restored.

But restored to what? And what kind of Aboriginal was I? Clearly, I was in a category of my own, understandable perhaps only to me. Up until now Aboriginality had equated with colour rather than specific racial background or cultural or social affiliation, although I recognised that would change with my newly acquired status. I had no first-hand experience of Aboriginal society. The only Aboriginal person I had ever known was Neville. And I had never been dispossessed, my people dispersed. Still, on my own terms, I knew how it felt to be Aboriginal. I had experienced the derision although, clearly, not economic or social disadvantage. From this perspective, claiming to be Aboriginal seemed completely natural because life had prepared me for it right from the outset.

I asked myself again if I was claiming an Aboriginal identity less because I truly believed in my Aboriginal descent, than because I just wished to identify as something. How much of my decision was motivated by the belief in my Aboriginality and how much by a need to belong? I found these questions perplexing. Clearly the fact that Aboriginality conferred a ready made identity was an important ingredient. Now, for the very first time, I could actually claim a race and identity. This made me feel complete and fulfilled in a way I had only imagined previously. However, I did feel Aboriginal, so it was a combination of both. Additionally, if I was to identify with any ethnic or social grouping then, on the basis of life experience, Aboriginals were the obvious choice. I didn't desire just to be anything. It was Aboriginal that I wanted to be. It was that particular background that naturally filled the void.

I also wondered if I was motivated by a sense of entitlement to an Aboriginal identity and a Commonwealth grant? Unquestionably there was an element of that. After all I had suffered for my colour. I knew what it felt like to be non-Anglo-Saxon and discriminated against. To that extent I felt that I had paid any relevant dues. I had earned the right to be Aboriginal. However, this wasn't my primary motivation. Overriding everything was my unwavering belief in my Aboriginal heritage. That belief had been inculcated throughout my life, based on the amalgam of my colour, what I believed myself, and what others had suggested. As for the financial benefits and entitlements the grant conferred, obviously they counted but were secondary. My driving force was identity.

A friend asked me why on earth I would choose to be 'black'? The question irritated me intensely. From my perspective it revealed a complete lack of understanding of somebody in my situation. I had never chosen to be 'black'. As far back as I could recall, it had been other people who had questioned my racial background and suggested that I must be Aboriginal. I had been tagged Aboriginal by others. Until this moment, it had never been something I had actively sought. Aboriginality and I had merely encountered one another early on. Being referred to as a 'coon', an 'Abo' or a 'boong' was as familiar to me as breathing, the same as it was for most indigenous Australians.

I thought about belonging to arguably the longest continuous culture on earth. The idea engendered pride. The fact that this was also the most disadvantaged group in the community also crossed my mind. I considered the appalling health and social problems evident in indigenous communities, symptomatic of the vast and unnatural dichotomy between ancient culture and modern Australia. I was aware of the disparity in health standards between indigenous and non-indigenous Australians and the gaping discrepancies which existed in mortality rates between the two groups. I knew that the infant mortality rate for Aboriginal Australians was three times the national average, the difference between indigenous and non-indigenous adult mortality rates equally disturbing. Incidences of diabetes, hepatitis B, circulatory system and eye disease were considerably higher for Aboriginals and they were admitted to hospital many times more frequently than other Australians. Then there were the intractable problems of alcohol and other drugs, symptomatic of the despair devastating the dispossessed and disadvantaged everywhere.

Soon after returning to Hobart I contacted Dick.

'Did you speak to your parents, Gordon?' he enquired.

'Yes, I did,' I replied. 'We discussed everything in detail. I'm not sure that Dad understands entirely. My gut instinct tells me he could well do without all this. Maybe deep inside he does prefer the idea of an Anglo-Saxon son. I really don't know.

'However, Mum's attitude couldn't have been more supportive. She was absolutely fantastic. She understands my situation because she's witnessed everything first-hand. Mum's view is that if I can't establish the truth, then I'm entitled to follow my heart.'

'Well, what are you going to do?' he asked. This time there was no hesitation in my reply.

'I'm going to be Aboriginal from now on,' I responded.

A week or so later, Dick took me down to speak to the Aboriginal study grant people in the Commonwealth Department of Education. Given his involvement in Aboriginal education, Dick knew the relevant bureaucrats and the procedure for applying for a grant. I remained apprehensive about how the authorities would view my claim. Would I meet the selection criteria? Would I really be entitled to receive a grant? As things turned out, I needn't have worried. Following Dick's explanation of my circumstances, I signed a form stating my belief in my Aboriginal descent. For the first time, officially at least, I had become Aboriginal.

I suppose it was ironic that I had become Aboriginal in Tasmania, the only state where it was commonly believed Aboriginal people had died out completely. The historical record of white Tasmanians in relation to the treatment of Aboriginals was appalling. In the 1820s the so-called Black Line mobilised the entire population for six weeks as several thousand men, including 500 troops, walked across the island in an unsuccessful effort to drive the surviving clans into the south-west corner. The operation cost 30 000 pounds, equivalent to half the colonial government's annual expenditure. Such activity steadily destroyed the sixty or so Aboriginal groups which recognised distinct geographical boundaries, spoke different dialects and formed nine major tribes. Now an Aboriginal renaissance was evident, with those who declared themselves to be of Aboriginal descent rejecting claims that the Tasmanian Aboriginal race was extinct. Aboriginal leaders delivered impassioned speeches supporting the existence of Tasmanian Aboriginals, in contrast with earlier claims by many people that the race had been extinguished with the death of Truganini in 1876.

Again I reflected on my own mixed blood, privileged background and exceptional circumstances. What did it mean for a middle-class, ex-Scotch College boy like me to be identifying with a group of people totally removed from his own upbringing and anyone he knew? I was prepared to find out.

CHAPTER 13

Becoming a
Diplomat

My newly acquired status didn't manifest itself in any obvious way. I didn't involve myself with Aboriginal activists or Aboriginal organisations. At such a small university there wasn't much activity visible and Dick didn't direct me anywhere in particular. In any case, as state director of the World University Service, an organisation which raised funds for community programs in developing countries, I was already heavily involved in extra-curricular pursuits on campus. Our activities included raising money for teacher training in Bangladesh and providing assistance to international students on campus.

Apart from that, I didn't feel any need to involve myself actively in Aboriginal affairs. I had been looking for an identity, a sense of completeness, the ability to say for the very first time precisely who I was. After all, that had been my motivation for assuming an Aboriginal identity; that had been more important than anything. For now I was just feeling my way, getting used to who I had become and thinking about the future generally. I expected that I would become more involved with time.

I had a succession of part-time jobs after leaving Tasmania and my employment history was chequered, to say the least. So extensive was my litany of part-time positions that I can't even remember them all. Tutoring secondary school students in English, marking university psychology papers, delivering mobile television rentals, lengthy stints as a wine waiter and barman. I delivered meals on wheels to the sick and elderly in Melbourne's inner suburbs, worked in a music agency booking bands and performed as a disc jockey in a city discotheque. It was also during these unsettling years that Dad died, finally victim of his damaged heart.

Gran Brodrick was insistent that I needed to settle down and I recognised that my unfocused lifestyle was leading nowhere. But finding something to devote myself to in the long term was easier said than done. Employment options weren't exactly prolific for a twenty-eight-year-old arts graduate with psychology and English majors and preliminary postgraduate work in Indian studies, which I undertook at Melbourne University, my interest ignited after backpacking around northern India. Only two possibilities occurred to me: teaching and the diplomatic service.

Teaching was definitely out of the question; it didn't fire my imagination. But a professional life involving Australian foreign policy, travel and the opportunity to experience different cultures sounded ideal. I knew that a handful of Melbourne University Indian studies graduates had succeeded in joining the diplomatic stream of the Department of Foreign Affairs. And while the notion of becoming a Canberra bureaucrat was something I had never seriously entertained, there was one brief moment during another visit to the Indian sub-continent in my mid-twenties which had lodged in my mind.

Travelling with Kay by rickshaw on a scorching Delhi day, we crossed the city's Chanakyapuri diplomatic district, resplendent with opulent embassies. Sweaty brown workers ambled lazily tending immaculate gardens. As a sleek, black embassy vehicle cruised past, Kay poked her head outside, eyeing the car enviously. 'Wouldn't it be wonderful,' she sighed. I agreed with her. Recovering from a bout of Delhi belly, Kay's lust for comfort was magnified by the reality of the filthy communal toilet awaiting us back at the hotel.

'You should be aware that competition is fierce and the chances of success virtually nil,' the university careers counsellor advised when I sought information about the Foreign Affairs application and selection process. 'Only a tiny percentage of applicants get in, so don't raise your hopes too high. You'll be more than lucky to crack the first interview. Most applicants don't make it that far. Those jobs are like gold.'

'But how many people do they actually take?' I enquired.

'I can't give you a precise figure,' she replied. 'I understand they accept about twenty each year, sometimes a few more, sometimes less. Between seven hundred and a thousand graduates apply annually, many with honours degrees. But there were some years during the 1970s when they didn't recruit any trainees at all.'

Leaving with the application form in my hand, I couldn't have felt less hopeful. My spirits slumped even further when I examined the document thoroughly. A plethora of information and supporting documentation was sought including university results, referee reports, personal references and a comprehensive statement about what individual applicants could offer Foreign Affairs. The document explained that many successful applicants possessed honours degrees and warned about the competitive nature of the application process.

Those whose applications survived initial screening and who scored sufficiently well in the public service graduate examination and an accompanying written general knowledge test, progressed to the interview stage; a small percentage. The applicants who survived the interview then advanced to the final round, an intensive two-day selection exercise comprising discussion seminars, written and oral examinations and a public speaking exercise. Short-listed applicants from all states and territories were flown to Sydney for this make-or-break final assessment.

Those lucky enough to get this far were then subject to security checks. An acquaintance who had once made it through to the final round before being eliminated told me that the entire selection process lasted around nine months. Being realistic, my chances of winding up anywhere near this deciding stage appeared remote to say the least; about as likely as winning a lottery.

Nevertheless, following several redrafts, I rushed off my application one day before the closing date. In addition to stressing a serious interest in politics and international relations, I referred to my knowledge of other cultures, my background in Indian studies and my extensive travels throughout Asia. A few weeks later, I received a proforma letter advising my application was under consideration and that, as an initial step, I would be required to sit the public service graduate entry examination. I had survived the first hurdle.

When advice arrived that I had passed the public service exam and an accompanying general knowledge test, I felt surprised and cautiously optimistic. The letter I received advised that as a next step I would be interviewed by the director of the Foreign Affairs diplomatic training course and other departmental officials.

The day before the interview one of my university lecturers, who had applied successfully for Foreign Affairs several years previously, provided me with a handy tip. 'Remember Gordon, diplomats are team players. Whatever else the interview team is seeking, they'll be looking for moderate people, individuals who won't rock the boat. No foreign service values brash, independent thinkers. Team players are what they're after. Try to project that kind of image. Convey it in your answers. Make sure you dish up what they're hoping to hear. Remember to display moderation in everything. That's the key. Don't lose sight of that.'

A year or so later when I read the written report on my interview, I was amused by the committee's comment that 'several times he mentioned the value of moderation, and overall gave the impression of an articulate and reasonable man who could argue a case convincingly'.

During the interview I was grilled on all sorts of things: growing up in Melbourne; family life in Kew; Scotch College; university experiences; the social circles in which I moved; my hobbies and interests. I was even asked to identify which national personalities I admired most. I mentioned Dame Joan Sutherland — I'm not sure why — and Gary Foley, the Aboriginal activist.

Eventually, the panel broached the vital subject. 'We note from your application that as an Australian of Aboriginal descent, you've studied on a Commonwealth Aboriginal study grant,' ventured Mr Webb, the course director.

'Yes, that's right, although I'm adopted and my full racial background is unclear. I believe I'm of Aboriginal descent although, as you're aware, I didn't grow up in an Aboriginal environment.'

Mr Webb peered intently through his spectacles. 'As you know, we're interested in all aspects of applicants,' he advised. 'Your Aboriginality is only one element of the overall picture.' I fidgeted uneasily.

'Having said that, your Aboriginal background certainly interests us. You're probably aware that the Government is keen to attract Aboriginal Australians into all areas of the bureaucracy. No doubt you saw some of our advertising in the press or on the Melbourne University campus. I presume that's how you came to apply?'

'No,' I replied. 'I haven't seen a thing.'

'Did you know that no Australian of Aboriginal descent has ever been recruited into the diplomatic stream of the Department via our regular recruitment program?'

'No, I didn't,' I responded, feigning surprise. I would have been amazed to hear otherwise.

'Until now, we haven't discovered Aboriginal Australians with skills appropriate to foreign policy work. It's difficult to find Aboriginal people with the abilities we're seeking, and of the few who do have appropriate qualifications, virtually all seem more interested in working directly with their own people, which is of course entirely understandable. This year we've systematically targetted communities and institutions by advertising on campuses with significant numbers of Aboriginal and Torres Strait Islander students such as James Cook University in Townsville. We've also placed advertisements in Aboriginal and Torres Strait Islander publications.

'Regrettably, with the notable exception of yourself, of the sixty or so responses received from Aboriginal applicants this year, none of them possessed — how can I put it —' Mr Webb paused thoughtfully, 'academic qualifications and skills directly relevant to the Department and its foreign policy functions. Apart from yourself, we won't be interviewing any other Aboriginal applicants this year.'

This was hardly surprising. I knew first-hand how the system worked in relation to Aboriginals and Torres Strait Islanders. How many had been afforded the opportunity to develop the skills necessary to compete equally in a selection process such as this? I thought back to the early 1970s when I started university and the handful of Aboriginal students studying at the main university campuses in the country. What could be more revealing than the fact that almost two hundred years after European settlement, only a smattering of Aboriginal students were undertaking tertiary studies within Australia — there wasn't a single Torres Strait Islander.

My family background assumed centre stage in my mind as we continued our conversation. No one needed to remind me that I had only arrived at this interview courtesy of a privileged, distinctly un-Aboriginal, upbringing. I waited for him to state the obvious.

'Your application is of particular interest to us. There must be very few Australians with a similar profile. I mean, not too many Aboriginals grew up like you with professional parents who took them overseas and educated them at schools like Scotch College. Now, let's discuss your circumstances a little more,' said Mr Webb.

'Despite your lack of a traditional Aboriginal background, growing up in Kew and all that, you claim an Aboriginal background. Is that correct?'

'Yes,' I replied. I wondered if Mr Webb would ever change subjects.

'Your situation is quite special given the increasing importance of equal employment opportunity and positive discrimination towards indigenous Australians and other minority groups. I'm sure you're well aware of the enormous possibilities available in government to someone with your particular attributes.'

'Well, yes, it has occurred to me,' I acknowledged. Of course I knew that government departments and agencies were keen to attract the trickle of Aboriginal graduates entering the job market each year. To a panel of white male bureaucrats keen to attract adequately qualified Aborigines, an olive-skinned Scotch College boy like me was close to a dream come true.

I focused intently on what Mr Webb was saying. 'I presume you're aware that, although we'd be recruiting you strictly on the basis of your qualifications and abilities, inevitably your

Aboriginality would give you a higher profile than other applicants we might employ.'

'I'm sure I can handle any additional responsibilities that might arise,' I replied, trying to appear as nonchalant as possible. I'd consciously avoided exploiting my Aboriginality, partly because I didn't want to, partly because I realised I simply didn't need to.

As the interview moved steadily towards its conclusion, I hadn't a skerrick of doubt that I would be seeing Mr Webb again. Sure enough, a month or so later a letter arrived inviting me to participate in the final two-day program in Sydney. The program sounded daunting: two seminar discussions, a prepared talk, a written summary record of conversation, an economic interpretation exercise and general knowledge tests covering both international and Australian current affairs.

One of the seminar discussion topics was 'Australia's Historical Achievements and Shortcomings Over Two Hundred Years — As Australia approaches her Bicentennial, of what should she be proud and ashamed?'. This question offered an ideal opportunity to refer to the impact and effects of European settlement on Aboriginal Australia. It appeared tailor-made for me.

The night before the final selection exercise, I slept fitfully. Hauling myself out of bed the following morning, I downed several cups of coffee before heading for the airport and Sydney. In the plane, I rummaged through the papers I'd flung together to assist my final preparation. Employed full time in a restaurant in addition to studying, I hadn't found time to peruse them until now. I wondered how many other finalists might be doing precisely the same thing.

The formal proceedings began pleasantly enough with a morning tea on the terrace. Mr Webb approached immediately. 'Nice to see you, Gordon. I'm pleased you could make it. Best of luck. By the way, I wanted to let you know that your interview went extremely well although my colleagues considered I was excessively harsh on you. I do trust that wasn't the case. They claimed I was tougher on you than on anyone else.'

'I'm just pleased to be here,' I replied. 'Thanks for including me.'

One of the most daunting exercises during the two days was a five-minute talk, requiring considerable preparation, which each of us delivered before a panel. My topic was 'Human Rights in Foreign Policy', and pacing outside the examination room I waited anxiously for my name to be called. I felt uncomfortably on edge. That morning at breakfast I had sat next to one finalist who explained dejectedly how she had delivered her talk the previous day and completely stuffed it up. Inadequately prepared, she had run out of things to say, grinding to a halt several minutes into her presentation.

Suddenly I heard my name called. Anxiously, I entered the room where the selection panel was spread out behind a distant table. I'd been advised that a bell would be rung at the start and finish of the designated period, the panel emphasising the importance of not running over time. Nervously, I delivered my presentation, mercifully without major difficulty. Responding to questions afterwards, I linked human rights and indigenous Australians wherever possible. Clearly there were points to be gained in doing that. When the panel's questions were over, I felt indescribable relief. I appeared to have survived.

When the two days were up, it was difficult to assess how I'd done. Obviously better on some exercises than others, and the lack of time to prepare had been a problem. 'Everyone probably feels like that,' I reassured myself. When a letter arrived several weeks later advising that I had been selected, I could scarcely contain my delight. How proud Gran would be. Finally I was settling down.

CHAPTER 14

Revised Circumstances

From the outset, I felt challenged and stimulated by life in the Department of Foreign Affairs. Another world was being revealed to me. During the first few months, I was relieved that my Aboriginal background was never alluded to. Not because I didn't feel Aboriginal, but I was keen to avoid being used as a token — if that was what the Department had in mind.

Things changed dramatically as the result of a one-day Aboriginal cultural awareness program organised three months into our training. The course comprised presentations delivered by about half a dozen Aboriginal bureaucrats.

One member of the panel was a woman named Eleanor Bourke, whom I knew from the early 1970s when she was Aboriginal liaison officer at Melbourne University. Eleanor now headed the Aboriginal and Torres Strait Islander Section of the Department of Social Security developing policy and advising government on Aboriginal and Torres Strait Islander social welfare issues. Eleanor introduced me to the only other Aboriginal officers in the Department at the time: Jirra Moore from Wreck Bay on the New

South Wales south coast, and Stephen Hagen, a Queenslander. Both were on the panel.

Although I'd never met him, Stephen's father Jim was a senior and respected representative of his people and the first Aboriginal Australian to address the United Nations Human Rights Commission in Geneva. Both Jirra and Stephen had entered the Department on secondment from the Department of Aboriginal Affairs just a couple of months prior to my arrival.

This was my introduction to Canberra's Aboriginal community. Jirra and Stephen accepted me unreservedly and introduced me to other 'blacks' around Canberra, the majority employed within the bureaucracy. For the first time in my life I was participating actively in Aboriginal Australia. Aboriginality had infiltrated everyday life. Now it was part of me.

Contemplating further my situation, I realised that for the first time Aboriginality had now ceased to be based on colour. Its context had been redefined. From an Aboriginal perspective the colour of skin, eyes and hair had nothing to do with Aboriginality. And certainly, government and bureaucracy defined it differently, legislators having abandoned their genetically prescriptive classifications after governments had provided no less than sixty-seven separate definitions of what constituted an Aboriginal person. Now the accepted official definition of an Aboriginal person — that used by the Department of Aboriginal Affairs since the early 1970s — was 'someone of Aboriginal descent who identifies as such and is recognised by their Aboriginal community to be so'.

Strikingly, this definition did not refer to a specific genetic quantum, perhaps because, offensively to indigenous Australians, for almost a century colonial and state Aboriginal Acts endeavoured to impose biological definitions, establishing criteria based on percentages of Aboriginal blood. Clearly I met the first part of the definition although not the second. Still I wasn't alone in that. Due to displacement, dispersal and the removal of Aboriginal children from their parents, not all Aboriginals could claim a definite community.

Suddenly life had changed significantly. Where was I now? I was not white Anglo-Saxon and I did identify as Aboriginal despite no traditional or cultural Aboriginal heritage whatsoever. Where did that leave me? And what about the missing pieces? Clearly my perception of my racial background and Aboriginality were being redefined, although precisely how I was anything but sure. Why had life inflicted such distinctive circumstances upon me? I wondered if that would become clearer with time.

Soon I found myself closely involved in indigenous activities within the Department. There was a perception that I should participate and I was eager to comply. My first significant engagement came when foreign service training course participants visited Queensland to undertake a variety of projects and field trips. Divided into groups of half a dozen or so, one group researched the Queensland tourist industry, another gold mining around Charters Towers. Throughout the visit, we were accompanied by around twenty participants from various developing countries who joined our training course for a three-month period under Australian Government sponsorship.

Before leaving Canberra, I decided to organise a visit to Queensland Aboriginal reserves to observe the situation of Aboriginal people there first-hand. I was keen to learn everything I could and I knew a number of others were too. In arranging a visit to Palm Island, Mossman's Goobidi Bamanga Housing Cooperative and the Yarrabah mission outside Cairns, I liaised with Aboriginal community councils, arranging a comprehensive program which included calls on community leaders. My Aboriginal education was now vigorously underway. Not anticipating the appalling social conditions which we encountered, the overseas participants who accompanied me and two other Australian colleagues were shocked and horrified by the despair they often encountered.

Some time after the Aboriginal and Torres Strait Islander cultural awareness program, Eleanor Bourke and her husband Colin, later to head the Institute of Aboriginal and Torres Strait Islander Studies, approached me about establishing regular links between the National Aboriginal and Islander Club, with which they were closely associated, and the Department's twenty-eight other diplomatic trainees. It seemed an excellent idea. Colin and Eleanor were both keen to promote Aboriginal and Torres Strait Islander culture abroad and the proposed linkage would be beneficial. Soon after, the three of us launched a series of regular social functions which some training course participants attended, although not all. Significantly though, the first ever regular link between the Department and an Aboriginal organisation had been established. In terms of promoting Aboriginal affairs and interests within the Department, I felt I was doing some good.

During the course of the year, I also decided to encourage Aboriginal and Torres Strait Islander recruitment within the Department. It seemed indefensible that there weren't more indigenous officers. The universities were turning out more and more Aboriginal graduates and there was no longer any excuse for not achieving a credible presence within the bureaucracy, especially within a Department responsible for promoting Australia's image overseas. In my view, cranking up the numbers appeared straightforward, particularly given my acquaintance with the Bourkes. As assistant secretary heading the Employment and Training Branch within the Department of Aboriginal Affairs, Colin maintained a register of tertiary programs available to Aboriginals and Torres Strait Islanders and also kept track of indigenous tertiary students and graduates throughout the country.

To speed things along, I spoke to an officer within the Department's Staffing Section. Susan Sims listened attentively while I explained that if the Department was as keen as it claimed to increase Aboriginal employment levels, then the ideal person to contact would be Colin. I even provided a contact phone number. Susan assured me she would get in touch.

Several weeks later, I was disappointed to hear from Colin that no one from staffing had yet made contact. Once more I spoke to Susan to ensure things progressed. Again I received an assurance that somebody would definitely follow-up. No one ever did. It was to be another decade before a second Australian of Aboriginal or Torres Strait Islander background was recruited as part of the Department's diplomatic recruitment process.

As 1983 progressed, I found my situation increasingly difficult. Whether I liked it or not, both the Department and the Aboriginal community considered me a role model. I had acquired a significant profile. During the year, at the community's behest, I found myself accompanying a Miss NAIDOC finalist to the National Aboriginals' and Islander Day Observance Committee Ball, a major event celebrating the most important day of the year for indigenous Australians and their supporters. A variety of events were held nationally during NAIDOC Week to promote the cultural identity of Aboriginals and Torres Strait Islanders and the positive contribution made by indigenous Australians to the nation.

I was also interviewed on several occasions by Flo Grant, a Wiradjuri woman from central southern New South Wales, later secretary of the Aboriginal Church in Canberra. Flo, who subsequently became a friend, had her own show on Canberra community radio.

Sometimes I was invited to address young indigenous Aus-
ralians visiting Canberra about possible career paths on leaving
school and other aspects of their future. The first time I
participated I found the session depressing. Meeting with a group
of shy and reserved teenagers, the only one with any idea of what
she wanted to do was a girl who had been adopted by a white
family. She planned to be an air hostess.

On another occasion, John Dawkins, the finance minister and
later federal treasurer, who was married to an Aboriginal woman
at the time, attended a function to meet the Department's new
'Koori' diplomat. 'So you're the one,' he remarked sidling up to
meet me.

Before leaving Canberra at the end of the year on my first
posting to Nigeria, the Department of Aboriginal Affairs provided
me with a glowing letter of introduction to the Nigerian foreign
minister. While never using the letter, I was reminded again that I
was a role model with an expanding profile. Professionally, the
future couldn't have appeared any brighter.

Early in 1984, the director of the foreign service training course
asked if I would prepare an Aboriginal affairs program for use in
the course. Pleased to be asked, I prepared a program to be
chaired by Eric Willmot, principal of the Australian Institute of
Aboriginal Studies, later professor of education at James Cook
University and director-general of the South Australian Education
Department. Both academic and inventor, former stockman Eric
was an acclaimed speaker with a fascinating and eclectic background. Several years later he would be one of the first to
encourage me to write this book. I also recommended screening
several films. One, an ABC–BBC co-production titled *A Plain and
Sacred Right*, dealt with the dispute over mining in the West
Australian outback town of Noonkanbah and the Aboriginal
relationship to the land. The other, *The Broken Covenant*,

examined the work of a Sydney priest, Father Kennedy of Redfern, and explored the problems faced by urban Aboriginals. I also suggested that both Colin and Eleanor Bourke be included on a panel of four or five individuals.

Soon after the program, I received a letter from the training course director thanking me for my efforts. The trainees had been immensely impressed by Eric Willmot who gave a spellbinding performance linking the past, the present and the eternal. Quite a few of the Australian trainees had been shocked out of their complacency. The director went on to say he had found the program inspiring personally and would be retaining it for the following year. I definitely was doing some good.

Yet I kept worrying over the issue of where I stood now in relation to my Aboriginality. I had been accepted fully within both the Aboriginal community and the bureaucracy. The process couldn't have been any smoother. One or two individuals in the Aboriginal community did question my origins, although only one in a negative or aggressive way. After all, I couldn't say definitely where my 'mob' came from, could I? That was starting to make me feel uneasy. For the first time I was beginning to wonder precisely how Aboriginal I was. And plainly I was unable to say conclusively. My situation was beginning to make me feel increasingly uncomfortable.

For the first time I thought seriously about trying to find my natural parents. While I had always believed instinctively that they were decent people who would be delighted by my appearance, this was something I'd never felt ready for. It would upend my world and besides, I already had a family. I wasn't even certain how to go about it although Link-Up, the agency established by Coral Edwards and Peter Read in 1980, sprang instantly to mind. Coral, an Aboriginal writer and film-maker, had herself been a victim of separation. I'd seen several television reports about Link-

Up and its work, and heard Coral interviewed. Link-Up's primary function was to assist Aboriginal Australians who had been separated forcibly from their families as children and adopted out or raised in institutions or by foster parents, a practice which continued in New South Wales until after 1969.

I couldn't recall when I'd first learnt about that disgraceful chapter in Australian history, but for years I'd been aware that the treatment of Aboriginal children represented one of white Australia's most shameful misdeeds. In 1911 the New South Wales Aborigines Protection Board described Aboriginal children as a positive menace to the state and a 1915 amendment to the NSW Aborigines Protection Act empowered the Board to 'assume full control and custody of a child of any Aborigine in the interests of [its] moral or physical welfare'. No one knows how many Aboriginal children were stolen officially or what happened to them. Brothers and sisters were separated routinely by the white authorities, visits by parents were discouraged and children never returned home again. Records were inaccurate and, in many instances, simply not kept.

Coral and others like her had been spurred into action by the need for Aboriginal people to contact lost family members. I knew Link-Up had been extremely successful in reuniting families and in assisting and counselling people, who in many cases had been completely unaware of their background, through the process of adjusting to the realities of their Aboriginality. Many victims of separation had been damaged emotionally and psychologically and were ashamed of being 'black'. The organisation's task was colossal. I'd read that in New South Wales alone, an estimated ten thousand children had been forcibly removed by the Aborigines Protection Board and other government agencies. I'd also heard first-hand about the forced removal of Aboriginal children up until recent decades. I recalled vividly Jirra recounting how welfare officials would raid the mission at Wreck Bay where he grew up. It was an entirely different story to mine. It was shocking.

'Every time someone heard a vehicle the entire mission would become uneasy. The sound of a car could only mean a few things. The white manager returnin' home, the police arrivin' — they were authorised to take children too — the welfare, or one of the handful of 'blacks' who owned their own vehicle. The welfare people often drove old Vauxhalls. Not too many Holdens arrived at Wreck,' he chuckled.

'The best lookouts were the dogs. They went berserk whenever strangers appeared. Ya got to remember, too, that Wreck was a mission in every sense of the word. About three hundred 'blacks' on the mission itself and a few on the fringes in camps. We were completely segregated from the outside world. Not many strangers arrived. I hardly ever came in contact with whites growin' up. Our world was different.

'Often we'd be sittin' in the house when we'd hear a car. Fear and panic gripped everyone,' continued Jirra, his face animated as if living the moment anew. '"Quick, get out a here," Mum would yell, if on glancin' out the window, she established it was the welfare. All the kids'd scatter usin' the nearest exit, out the windows, out the door, racin' off barefoot through the tussock grass and on up the hill that backed our place, everyone headin' bush. It was somethin' shockin'. The hill provided a perfect vantage point. We could see what was goin' on. Sometimes there'd be fifteen to thirty kids up there. There were hills the other side, too, so there was always somewhere to escape.

'Sometimes we'd stay hidin' for a whole day or two. Build gunyahs. It was cold at Wreck in winter. Luckily there was plenty o' bush tucker. Lilli-pilli, pig face, yam, geebung, all kinds o' stuff. We loved the geebung. Do ya know it? Sweet little fruit smaller than grapes. Comes in all different colours: yella, green, red. We'd also tear the spikes off honey-suckle and suck the honey out. Another thing we'd do is make fires and poke branches inside the hollow trunks where bees made their hives to smoke 'em out and collect bush honey.

'Wreck's surrounded by bays so there was abalone and oysters and fish to spear too. Heaps o' tucker. We never went hungry. The fish was delicious wrapped in leaves and tossed in the coals. It was best, though, if ya rolled it in clay and then placed it in the ashes. Later we'd break the clay open and the fish'd be all cooked inside. Often we rabbited too, caught 'em in traps or speared 'em. We had a marvellous time. It was shockin' goin' back home though, wonderin' who'd been taken this time round. We couldn't count up among ourselves to work that out because all the kids'd run off in different directions, so ya were never sure who was where. When ya got back though ya didn't need to ask because ya knew immediately. You could hear the mothers sobbin'. I'll never forget that. Terrible.'

But what touched my own heart most poignantly about the forced removal of Aboriginal children was finding Neville Austin — the Aboriginal boy I had known during my Scotch days and the only Aboriginal person I ever met while growing up. He had grown into a dignified and successful man and I listened and wept silently as he explained, in a voice devoid of bitterness, how he had been removed from his mother at five months of age when she had taken him to Melbourne's Royal Children's Hospital with a chest infection, and how when growing up he had never understood what mothers and fathers even were. As a child, The Gables had been the only place he had thought of as home and in which he had ever felt safe and secure. He also told me how at sixteen years of age he had learnt for the first time that he had a mother. At that age he was still to hear officially about his Aboriginal background.

This special person in my life who, unbeknown to him, I had never forgotten, also talked about foster parents who abused him and how he was frequently told that he was dirty and that if he drank milk it would make his skin lighter. He went on to describe his joy when at eighteen years of age he finally met his mother, a Gunditjmara woman from Victoria's western district, who had pleaded unsuccessfully with the authorities for more than a decade and a half for his return and who regularly sent letters and birthday and Christmas cards which he never received. Neville's mother died five years after their reunion having taught him to let go of the past and having put aside her grief to combat his. He treasured those special years they had finally spent together and later, when government policies changed, he finally obtained those tokens of her love which he cherished more than anything.

Now as an adult, Neville works as an Aboriginal family support worker, helping others like himself. He told me that he had learnt to live not only with his own pain but also with his mother's, referring sadly to the incalculable price which both of them had paid.

CHAPTER 15

Nigeria

In early 1984, eleven months after joining the Department, I headed off to Lagos on a two-year posting as third secretary at the Australian High Commission in Black Africa's most populous city. I was only the third person from my intake to be posted and had no real idea what lay ahead. The fact that the Nigerian capital was one of the least popular destinations in the Foreign Service didn't worry me a bit. Lagos had been my first choice. I was seeking an African experience and Nigeria would certainly provide that. Also Lagos seemed an appropriate post for an Aboriginal officer.

Third secretaries boasted a less than inspiring track record in Lagos. One of my predecessors had been killed in a plane crash flying into the city at the start of his posting, while another had fallen to his death from a hotel room window.

The junior of three policy officers, my primary responsibility was to report on internal political and foreign policy developments in Nigeria, and Niger and Gabon — two west African francophone countries for which the High Commission also held responsibility. My tasks also included administering Australia's student program in west Africa and liaising with the Nigerian press. It was an exciting time. Settling into my new environment, there weren't too many friends with whom I would have willingly swapped jobs.

Domestic life in Nigeria was made considerably easier thanks to Gilbert Dossou, my steward from the neighbouring Republic of Benin. Keen to improve my French, I decided to employ a French-speaking Beninois rather than a Nigerian. Many expatriates in Lagos employed Beninois who crossed the neighbouring border, usually illegally, to seek work in wealthier Nigeria. Gilbert spoke only his tribal language and French, and insisted on calling me Monsieur instead of Gordon, despite my repeated requests.

Gilbert disliked me spending too much time in the sun. In his view it made me excessively dark. Gilbert preferred a light-coloured Monsieur. I suspected most stewards would have thought the same. Gilbert was forever telling me that white people were superior to blacks. I'd reply that was rubbish, that colour made no difference whatsoever, even though experience had taught me otherwise. Gilbert imagined he was speaking to the greatest idiot on earth.

'Monsieur just take a look around the house,' he'd say indulgently. 'Who invented the television? Who invented the stereo? What about the fridge and the freezer? Who has more money? Blacks or whites?'

'Don't be absurd,' I'd reply. 'Lots of black people are extremely successful. And as for money, there's heaps of black people who have more money than me.'

'Whatever you say Monsieur,' he'd reply disbelievingly.

One night during one of these frequent conversations that led nowhere, Diana Ross appeared on the television. 'What about her Gilbert?' I enquired. 'She's black and she earns an absolute fortune.'

'She's not black,' he replied. 'Not black like me.'

We argued back and forth a little longer. Gilbert remained unconvinced. The Africans often talked about someone I would consider black as being 'light'. Until then I'd never really thought about that particular colour being relative. However, in a place where black meant as black as you could imagine, colour took on a completely different meaning. Not in a million years was I ever going to convince Gilbert that someone like Diana Ross was genuinely black. Two years later, I'd made no progress whatsoever in persuading him that black was as worthwhile as white and that colour was unimportant. Gilbert remained convinced about my foolishness in this area. His thinking hadn't shifted an inch — but then again neither had mine. We both viewed the situation according to our respective backgrounds and contrasting experience.

CHAPTER 16

The Search

In the autumn of 1986 I returned to Canberra, the national capital, decidedly dull after the excitement of west Africa. I found myself missing my Nigerian friends and vibrant bazaars teeming with traders hawking their wares. Most of all I felt a disquiet within myself. I realised that as alien as Canberra felt, my reluctant return was not the cause of my frustration and unhappiness. During my time in Nigeria I had been confronted constantly by questions of colour and race. Now my own circumstances were beginning to haunt me. The experience of living in a black culture had affected me a great deal, provoking me to dig even deeper into my own background. I realised I would never really be satisfied with myself until I tracked down my natural mother and established definitely the truth about my racial background.

I had become uncomfortable with my racial status. For the first time I felt an irrepressible urge to establish precisely how Aboriginal I really was. After more than three decades, the time had arrived to confront the truth. No longer could I continue feeling uncertain and incomplete. As well, 1988 and the bicentennial loomed with all of its connotations for Aboriginal Australians. It would be important to clarify my identity before that auspicious date, particularly if the Department had a special role in mind for me.

Although I didn't know exactly how to go about it, I'd heard about various adoption organisations and people who assisted adoptees trying to find natural parents. I phoned Auntie Rose to seek her help. She seemed the natural place to start, although I felt more than a bit uncomfortable asking my mother's close friend — the woman who had arranged my adoption — for advice about how to track down my natural mother. It seemed like betraying the family, violating something sacred. I had to keep reminding myself that I shouldn't feel guilty.

'Now you're really sure you want to go ahead with this, Gordon?' queried Auntie Rose. 'You've definitely made up your mind?'

'Of course,' I responded bravely, 'I've got to find her. There's no longer any choice. I need to establish the truth. I have to find out precisely how Aboriginal I am.' We both paused. I could sense Auntie Rose considering how to advise me.

'Listen Gordon, I'm suspicious of some women who do this kind of work, but there's one person in whom I have absolute faith. Her name is Margaret Campi, I've known her for years. She's discreet and reliable. I respect her a great deal. You won't find anyone better.'

Hanging up the phone, I glanced down at the notepad on which I'd scribbled Margaret's name and number. It was an uncomfortable feeling, confrontational. This name and number might prove the crucial link to my disrupted past. Could Margaret Campi really lead me to my natural mother? It all seemed unreal, a ridiculous pipedream. In any case, who was this Colette Darcy? Did she even exist?

Clasping Margaret's name and phone number, I felt overwhelming panic. This was no longer a game. I was finally about to start searching. Either I had to move quickly and resolve this dilemma once and for all, or cast it aside altogether. There was, of course, no real choice. My problem had already sapped inordinate energy, preoccupying me constantly. Until it was solved I felt I couldn't move ahead with my life. Still, I delayed calling Margaret for a few days, stealing time to muster the requisite courage. Finally, apprehensively, I phoned one evening after work. Margaret sounded direct but sympathetic, a combination to inspire confidence.

Margaret listened quietly to the little I knew about my mother: her name and that at the age of twenty-three she had come from Sydney to Melbourne to have her baby. I mentioned how Mum had told me in my early teens that Colette had named me Paul before surrendering me for adoption. These fragments added up to three tangible facts about my mother, a name, an age, and the city she allegedly came from, but no firm proof that any of it was true. All the same, Margaret responded positively to the information which I provided. At least I had a name which meant she knew where to start.

'Hold on a minute, will you. I just want to check my computer,' announced Margaret unexpectedly. 'I've got thousands of names of both relinquishing mothers who want to make contact with their lost children and adoptees who are searching for their natural mothers.'

Fear and panic gripped me. I wasn't ready for this. I needed more time. Time to prepare mentally and emotionally. I mean, what if Colette's name did turn out to be listed and I discovered my mother straight off, just like that? While desperate to find her, this was terrifyingly quick, unmanageably so. Anxiously I awaited Margaret's return.

'Sorry Gordon, unfortunately she's not there,' advised Margaret a few minutes later. 'She hasn't indicated she wants to make contact with you, although that doesn't mean anything. Maybe she doesn't know about the register. Thousands of mothers still don't.' I heaved an immense sigh of relief.

'You're going to have to head for the National Library to start searching for Colette's name in the NSW electoral records,' advised Margaret a moment later, focusing directly on the process that lay ahead. 'You're lucky. It's close to your work, isn't it, and that library will have them all. It holds state records stretching back forever. It's compulsory in all states to register on the electoral roll on turning twenty-one. If your mother was twenty-three when you were born, as she told the Queen Vic, she should be listed on the electoral records for 1950 and 1951, the two years preceding your birth. Given that we don't have an address, you'll just have to select an electoral sub-division at random and start from there. I know that doesn't sound particularly hopeful, but unfortunately there's no alternative. Be warned, you're in for a frustrating experience. This'll require determination. Still, if your mother provided the hospital with her correct name when you were born, we'll eventually track her down. That much I promise.'

'But how can you be so sure?' I replied dubiously. 'I mean, we don't even know if she provided her real name. To start chasing her now through the electoral records — how long is that going to take?'

'Yes, I know,' replied Margaret. 'Unfortunately, that's the way it is. There's simply no alternative. Don't worry Gordon, it'll take time, but eventually we'll find her. Anyway, it's good that there's work for you to do. All adoptees should participate in the search for their birth parents. I consider that important.'

The mere thought of the tedious process that lay ahead exhausted me already. At thirty-four, I was about to begin hunting for lost pieces of myself.

The following night, I headed for the National Library where a librarian guided me to the upstairs archives, brimming with shelves of leather bound electoral records dating back decades. The shelves stretched forever. Margaret and I had surmised that if my mother did in fact come from New South Wales, a possible scenario was that she could have been a Sydney resident from a working-class or lower middle-class background, perhaps a resident of Sydney's sprawling west. However, there were no guarantees and that profile was pure conjecture. Still, we had to start somewhere.

Unsure as to which volume to select, I scanned the shelves containing the 1951 records, the year preceding my birth. Working through electorates alphabetically, I spent several hours poring unsuccessfully over interminable lines of minuscule print in pursuit of Colette Darcy and an address. Although this was only the beginning, already I feared that I was unlikely to get anywhere. Where would this lead?

Unfortunately there was no alternative. I had to remain hopeful and focused on the task at hand. Returning dispiritedly the following evening, I wondered for how long I'd keep this up. I wasn't exactly renowned for seeing things through at the best of times, and what I was doing somehow seemed pointless. Already my heart baulked at searching, and mustering the requisite energy was proving difficult after an oppressive day at work. I wondered if it was even worth persevering. Not having finished the previous evening, I decided to struggle on with Lowe, an inner western electorate of which I'd never even heard, which included the suburbs of Burwood and Strathfield. It was pointless examining volumes incompletely.

As my eyes waded through the blur of names and addresses, a listing leapt out at me. Colette Darcy. Colette Darcy. What was this? I couldn't believe it! There actually was a Colette Darcy and I had discovered her on only my second night of searching! The address listed beside Colette's name was 22 Park Avenue,

Burwood; her occupation recorded as typist. After not even four hours' searching, perhaps I had discovered the person I was after. Maybe things were destined to work out positively after all. Still, was this the correct Colette Darcy — the only Colette Darcy that mattered from my point of view? That was the question. However my instincts told me there couldn't be all that many Colette Darcys resident in New South Wales.

The following morning I rang Margaret excitedly. 'Listen, I found her, I think I've found her,' I exclaimed.

Margaret shared my enthusiasm, agreeing that I may indeed have hit the jackpot. At the same time, she chastened me gently. 'But you haven't gone far enough,' she cautioned. I didn't understand what she was getting at. After all, I'd discovered a listing with the correct name. This woman could possibly be the Colette we were after. What did Margaret mean?

'Remember, we need to look for males,' continued Margaret. 'We're trying to establish that this is a family residence. We're talking about a twenty-three-year-old woman who most probably married after your birth. Most women eventually married in those days. Assuming Colette did also, her surname will be different. You need to look again for brothers at the same address, their names won't have changed. Colette's surname is Irish, so there's bound to be other siblings, we can trace her through them.' Finishing work, I raced out of the Department and headed for the National Library, across the parliamentary triangle.

Several more days' searching left me utterly confused. Although I found no other Darcys listed at 22 Park Avenue, Burwood, I did uncover about a dozen other residents with Anglo-Saxon and Irish surnames at the same address. Meat inspectors, fruiterers, fitters, clerks, female domestics, a table hand, an office cleaner, even a prison warder. The import of all that eventually dawned on me: 22 Park Avenue was a boarding house.

Bitterly disappointed that it wasn't Colette's family residence, I phoned Margaret who agreed instantly with my conclusion. 'There's only one thing left to do now Gordon. However, it's illegal. You need a copy of Colette Darcy's birth certificate. Unfortunately the only way to get that is to break the law, and I'm not going to suggest you do that. You'll have to decide for yourself what you're prepared to do. How far you're willing to go.' At this stage I didn't give a damn whether I broke the law or not. After all the law had complicated my identity.

To avoid compromising Margaret, I sought independent advice within the bureaucracy. An acquaintance working for Community Services confirmed what Margaret had told me: a copy of the birth certificate would be vital to finding my mother. 'If you're determined to track her down, this is how you should approach it,' I was advised off the record. 'Take a day off work and visit the office of the NSW Registrar of Births, Deaths and Marriages in Sydney to apply for a copy of the certificate. Whatever you do, don't say you're adopted, or you'll never get it. Remember you have no legal connection with your natural mother whatsoever and therefore no entitlement to her birth certificate. Why don't you say Colette is your mother, but that you were raised by relatives due to family problems. If they push, you could even say you never actually knew your mother, that an aunt or someone else brought you up, that your mother is now dead and that you've started researching family history. That's why you require the certificate. If you pay an urgent search fee, you should have the certificate within a couple of hours, provided of course that the Colette Darcy you discovered in the electoral records was in fact born in New South Wales. You've probably heard how archaic the births, deaths and marriages system is in Australia. There's no national coordination, responsibility lies with individual states. That means if you don't find her in New South Wales, you're going to have to apply separately to each state and territory which could take forever.'

Feeling apprehensive, I followed my acquaintance's 'unofficial' suggestion and travelled to Sydney the following week. I didn't mention to Margaret my decision to break the law. That could be addressed later. Unless I pushed ahead, I'd never know the truth. It was as simple as that.

Waiting nervously in a queue at the Registrar's office, I prepared myself for the requisite lies, my heart pounding as I listened to those ahead of me being questioned. As a public servant myself, I knew the clerks were trained to probe thoroughly to ensure applicants' claims to certificates were legitimate. Some people requested birth certificates illegally in order to obtain passports.

'Colette Darcy is your mother, is that correct?' the young woman behind the counter asked when my turn arrived, her manner intense.

Never a good liar, I faltered. 'Well yes, but I'm adopted,' I blurted out unintentionally. As the import of what I had said hit home, I could scarcely believe what I had done.

'I'm sorry,' replied the woman. 'In that case you have no entitlement to her certificate. She's not legally your mother. I'm afraid I can't help.'

Dumbfounded, I stared dejectedly towards the woman. Desperate to start anew, the moment had passed irretrievably. I'd blown it on the first crucial question. Turning despondently, I headed for the door, berating myself all the way.

When I recounted everything, Margaret couldn't believe my woeful effort. I would need to try again. That would have to wait though; days off work could be arranged only occasionally.

Re-entering the same office a couple of weeks later, I couldn't believe my eyes. Only one person on duty: the very same woman.

For several hours I dallied, strolling in and out in the hope that the woman would go to lunch which she never did. Eventually, accepting there was nothing I could do except hope she wouldn't remember me from our previous encounter, I joined the queue crawling towards the counter. This time around there was no problem whatsoever. Not a glimmer of recognition. Flawlessly delivering my script, I paid the urgent search fee and left to unwind outside. Returning a few hours later, I departed triumphantly clutching Colette Darcy's birth certificate.

CHAPTER 17

The Certificate

I devoured every word of the certificate. Margaret had told me that older brothers and sisters were routinely listed as previous issue on birth certificates. In our case we were seeking an older brother should one in fact exist. That represented the most direct route to Colette. My heart sank immediately. The certificate advised no previous issue which meant Colette was the eldest child, our worst case scenario. Not only did no brothers exist, there wasn't even an older sister we could pursue. For all I knew, Colette could be an only child.

However, the certificate did provide several important snippets of information. From it I learnt that Colette Mary Darcy — the middle name I hadn't known previously — was born on 29 May 1929 at Talgarno Private Hospital, Port Kembla, in the Municipality of Central Illawarra. Forty-one years old when Colette arrived, Charles Darcy, her salesman father, had been born in Carlton, Victoria. On 7 February, one year before Colette's birth, Charles had married Moira Ward in Perth, Western Australia. Moira had been born in Marrickville in Sydney's industrial west. Witnesses to Colette's birth were a Doctor Wilkinson and Nurse H. Wilson.

As usual, Margaret listened to all I had to say, before proposing something that sounded so far-fetched I burst out laughing. 'Charles Darcy ...', she mused. 'Born in Carlton ... Darcy ... There probably aren't too many of them. These Irish families usually stick together. I'm going to look for Darcys in the Melbourne phone directory. I'll send a form letter to those I come up with.'

'But what on earth is this letter going to say?' For the first time I wondered whether Margaret might not be the supersleuth I had imagined.

Margaret appeared surprised by my naivety. 'That's obvious, isn't it? I'll claim that I'm a Darcy, and that as part of researching family history I'm seeking information about Charles Darcy, a distant relative born in Carlton.'

'And who in his right mind is going to reply to that?'

'Oh, I've done this heaps of times before,' replied Margaret unperturbed. 'You'll be surprised. I was when I began this work. Amazingly, people do respond. I know what I'm doing. This method usually works. I've got a standard letter on my word processor here at home which I'm able to amend as necessary. I'll mail the letters over the next few days.'

I was staggered to find Margaret's prediction proved correct. Contacting the forty or so Darcys listed in the Melbourne directory, Margaret received responses from around three-quarters, including two relatives of Charles.

One was an old spinster first cousin who didn't know much about him. However, a second cousin, Bernard Darcy, proved more useful. Margaret found Bernard suspicious when they spoke on the phone. Hardly surprising, I thought. However, Bernard did inform Margaret that Charles Darcy had died in 1956 and was buried in the public cemetery in Brighton, the Melbourne bayside suburb where Margaret lived and where Mum had grown up and her immediate relatives remained.

'I think I'll take a peek at Charles Darcy's grave,' commented Margaret not long afterwards. 'You never know, maybe I can find out something, a clue from the tombstone, or something hidden in the cemetery records. It's worth a shot.'

By now we were both feeling increasingly frustrated. Despite having uncovered considerable information about Colette Darcy, we still didn't know for certain whether or not she was in fact my mother, although instinct assured us we were on the right track. However, after several months searching, in terms of actually finding her, we hadn't progressed far at all.

The same day Margaret visited the cemetery, I headed up to Sydney to investigate 22 Park Avenue, Burwood. I had no idea what I would uncover, but wanted to snoop around. Maybe there would be neighbours who could tell me something. At the very least, it would give me a feel for where this woman had once resided.

Until now I had only ever had direct contact with one location in Sydney's west. Coincidentally, that had also been in Burwood. The year I joined the Department of Foreign Affairs as a diplomatic trainee I had moved from Melbourne to Canberra. In common with other colleagues, I frequently fled to Sydney on weekends to escape the national capital. Usually I travelled up with two other trainees, one of whom we would drop at her boyfriend's apartment in Burwood. That was my only encounter with Burwood or anywhere else in Sydney's west.

Journeying out to Burwood by train from Sydney's Central Station, I wondered how to find Park Avenue. Strolling down the suburb's main shopping drag, I sought directions along the way. The shopping and central business district was already familiar —

we drove through it routinely to reach my colleague's boyfriend's flat. Moving down the street, I drew closer to the street I knew already. A woman advised that Park Avenue was next on the left. Arriving at the street corner, I realised that Park Avenue was the same street where we dropped our colleague on Friday evenings, collecting her again on Sundays for our return together to Canberra. It was too uncanny for words. Rounding the corner, I ventured up the street.

To my utter amazement, 22 Park Avenue was next door to where my colleague's boyfriend lived. I couldn't begin to count how many times I'd stood directly out front, helping unload her bags from the boot of the car. The coincidence was extraordinary. The only address in western Sydney I'd ever visited, and my mother, if Colette Darcy was indeed my mother, had lived next door while I grew inside her.

By now I was certain. Colette simply had to be the person I was after. Fate was drawing us together. In a way I felt as though I'd already penetrated her life as she had mine. However, the boarding house at 22 Park Avenue had vanished long ago, replaced by a cream brick sixties-style apartment block. More than thirty years on, there were no clues to Colette's whereabouts. Her scent had grown cold.

Margaret didn't discover much either. Charles Darcy's unmarked grave revealed nothing and the cemetery records shed no new light. What struck me as extraordinary, though, was the idea of a woman whom I had never even met, sitting beside the grave of someone who might conceivably be my grandfather, pondering what she and I should do next.

CHAPTER 18

Margaret's Story

By now, I was fascinated with Margaret. My search was the most important event of my life, yet this new and crucial player effectively remained a stranger. Who on earth was she? I decided to visit Melbourne to meet the voice on the phone. Arriving, I was taken aback when Margaret opened the door. Slender and elegant, there was something quite captivating about her. She was nervous too, a rapid speaker. I sensed she ran on adrenalin. Over coffee, Margaret mentioned that she knew Mum. They still participated together on a Victorian state government adoption committee. Although I hadn't known anything about that when I began my search, Mum had subsequently explained this special connection to me.

Knowing nothing of her story, I was intrigued to find out how Margaret started in the adoption business. Margaret told me that she was adopted herself, talking about how she had found her own mother, and how she had been drawn subsequently to helping others unite. Margaret had been adopted as a month-old baby. There had been another adopted daughter in the family. 'We were the only two. I was five and my sister three when Mum, who was finally pregnant for the first time, told us we were adopted,' said Margaret. 'Mum was of English background, my adoptive father Estonian. Another natural child followed later. My mother always told me that when she decided to adopt she looked at lots of children but chose me because I smiled at her. That's impossible of course. Babies don't smile. Maybe I was full of wind!' chuckled Margaret.

'My life changed dramatically after the natural children were born. I was made to leave school at fourteen and, around the same time, my younger adoptive sister was forced to leave home and work as a children's nurse on a property at Three Springs, in northern Western Australia. She married at seventeen and after nine miscarriages, eventually adopted two children.

'Life for the two natural children was very different. Both finished school, and my brother went on to teach. When I turned sixteen I asked about my natural mother. Mum told me her correct name and that she came from Western Australia. She also told me that my natural mother had married a man named Tang, from Chidlow in rural Western Australia. The spelling turned out to be incorrect. It was Jigsaw, Western Australia, who found out years later. Jigsaw is an organisation that helps natural parents and adoptees reunite. They noticed that the correct name, almost identical but with an 'e', was listed directly below on the electoral roll. Jigsaw identified it immediately as the correct name from the address.

'Anyhow, soon after Mum had provided me with the name, I went to see the family doctor and told him I wanted to find my mother. He agreed to help, but told me to think about it carefully for a week or so. However, when I went back, he made me go home and repeat to myself that I couldn't hurt my adoptive parents. He made me feel guilty, as if I was being ungrateful and disloyal. Because of that, I didn't take it any further then, but I never forgot.

'Eventually I got a job travelling around Western Australia as an exchange supervisor for the Postmaster General's Department. That's how I met my husband who was a mining engineer. I eventually married Ric in Melbourne but went back to Perth to stay with my adoptive mother while I was having my first child. Because Ric and I lived in Melbourne, I paid for my adoptive mother to visit from Perth eighteen times in twenty-one years. She couldn't have afforded to pay for herself. Ric was of Italian origin and his people were very family minded. They were curious about my background and that I knew nothing about my natural parents. The need to look for my mother resurfaced. The fact that I had young children certainly had something to do with it. It was as if I had to find out for them too; to know where they were coming from. At forty-four, I finally wrote to Jigsaw in Victoria. They replied, but weren't overly positive. They made everything sound awkward and difficult. Around the same time, I read in the *Women's Weekly* that Jigsaw had started in Perth. I wrote off and joined the Western Australian branch.

'A lot of things led me to my mother at the same time. Soon after joining Jigsaw, my adoptive mother in Perth had a stroke. I hurried over to see her. Unaware that I'd already contacted Jigsaw, out of the blue Mum asked if I wanted to look for my natural mother and offered to help. She didn't need to do anything though, because two days after returning to Melbourne, Jigsaw phoned from Perth to say they'd found my mother. Her name was Thelma Black. As is so often the case, my natural mother knew instinctively what the Jigsaw call was about. "Does 20 December 1935 mean anything to you?" they asked. "Yes," she replied. "You've been looking for me for six months, haven't you?"

'After I first spoke to my mother I felt reborn. I could lift my head up and tell people who I was. I felt an enormous sense of confidence. Something extraordinary happened during that first phone call with my mother. She asked me where I'd lived as a child and I told her Inglewood/Mount Lawley. "What street?" she asked. "Sixth Avenue," I replied. "I lived in Fourth," she told me. "Not on the corner of Robinson Street?" I gasped. "Yes! How did you know that?" she queried. "That house haunted me. I could never walk past it as a child without my mother. I imagined a witch lived there. I had to pass by there to get to school. Mum used to have to meet me by the lane at the back. I must have been six. For some reason it stopped bothering me when I was about ten." "I left there in '45 when my husband got back from the war," my mother commented. "That must have been about the same time you stopped feeling scared," she added softly.

'It was while all this was going on that I decided to help other people. I wanted to give something back. Others had done my search, and now it was my turn to help. I'd been in mothers' clubs and all that sort of thing, but this was far more important to me. Regardless of what any law says, as far as I'm concerned everyone has the right to know where they come from. Who in their right mind's going to argue with that? That's why I don't charge anyone I help for my time and effort. I only claim tangible expenses — telephone calls, stationery, stamps, that sort of thing. Nothing else.

'I initially started working in adoption by joining Jigsaw, where I learnt to do searches. Jigsaw had about ten thousand names and dates of birth listed on its computer, which was a fantastic resource. We also used the old Sands and McDougall directories for Victoria. They aren't published anymore, so the information is out of date. However, they're still invaluable. They tell you where people lived and where they moved. A directory was produced annually for over one hundred years.

'Eventually, I ended up on the Jigsaw committee and was vice-president for two years from '82 to '84. We had around eight hundred and fifty members then and were growing. Jigsaw was instrumental in reforming the Victorian legislation in 1984 to allow natural parents and adoptees to make contact with one another. It was an active, exhausting time; lots of public meetings and lobbying politicians. I worked at least forty hours a week for no salary. In fact, it cost me money to be involved.

'In November the following year, my natural mother came over from Western Australia to stay with us in Melbourne for six weeks. That was very difficult. She never stopped talking about her guilt. A few weeks into the visit I thought I'd have to ask her to leave. I couldn't stand the intensity of it all. Finally, I decided to regard her as a regular visitor, keep calm and avoid going overboard. I had to learn to respect her guilt. It was better after that. When my natural mother returned to Perth she and my adoptive mother saw each other a few times. Unfortunately, there wasn't a great deal of love between them.

'My instincts about my adoptive mother's feelings for me proved to be correct. When she died in 1983, she named her two natural children as beneficiaries in her will. The will had been written seven years before I found my natural mother. I felt terribly wounded by not being named. Nothing to do with the money. Just that I'd always been a caring daughter.

'Anyhow, enough of all that. Since I started doing searches I guess I've helped around one hundred and fifty people, although I've never really counted. It would be interesting to know. I didn't realise all this would grow as it has, so I never kept tabs.

'In '85, following the changes to state legislation in Victoria, state community service authorities asked me to help train their staff in searching. I also helped non-governmental organisations. It was around that time that I became involved with the state standing committee on adoption and alternative families, the one your Mum's on. The committee includes medical people, adoption agency representatives, the Department of Community Services, Aboriginal welfare authorities — all kinds of people.

'Nowadays, I'm one of only three independent counsellors in Victoria. I do searches, make contacts and also mediate between the parties involved. Usually I have around fifty clients at any given time. It's all word of mouth. They hear about me in different ways. Just like you did. Things being as they are, adoptees wanting to find their natural parents are forced to contact people like me. Despite the fact that the law has been changed, there's still an eleven-year wait for birth certificates which is ridiculous. Who's prepared to delay that long?

'Last week was a pretty average week. I told a forty-nine-year-old he was adopted and that he had a blood brother he didn't even know about. I also had to tell a sixty-one-year-old that he was adopted. At that age, they can hardly believe it. Something sadder happened too. I took a fifty-nine-year-old woman to meet her eighty-one-year-old Jewish mother. The woman hadn't known her mother was Jewish. The mother spoke to us through the door for thirty minutes. She wouldn't invite us in. Said she was too old and too ugly to be bothered. As a young girl, the mother had been charged with immoral conduct for becoming pregnant under-age. The authorities sent her to the Good Shepherd Convent in Bendigo for five years. Unbeknown to the mother, her daughter was sent to the same home where, despite her mother signing the papers to permit adoption, she remained for twenty-five years. For some reason no one ever adopted her. The young children there were paraded on Sundays for prospective adoptive parents to pick and choose. Of course the mother believed, albeit incorrectly, that her daughter had been adopted out long ago. No one ever bothered to tell her the truth. Maybe it was just a bureaucratic oversight. Probably things just got muddled up. Who knows. Anyhow, for three years they were in the same home at the same time and the poor things never even knew. You know some girls never left those homes. A few remained in places like the Good Shepherd Convent in Abbotsford for up to sixty years. They couldn't cope with the idea of returning to the outside world.'

Never having heard anything like what Margaret was recounting, I listened spellbound. Hers was an extraordinary life. Now I understood her directness.

CHAPTER 19

Answered Prayers

When I next spoke to Margaret I could detect impatience in her voice. 'We're not progressing fast enough, are we Gordon?' she commented. I could only agree. This searching process was proving frustrating beyond words. Although we were both convinced that the Colette Darcy we now knew so much about was in fact my mother, we didn't seem to be any closer to finding her. Still, we hadn't yet completely exhausted all avenues. There was at least one thing left to try.

'I've been told that you can apply for a five-year marriage search in all states of Australia,' I told Margaret. 'As you said when we first started searching, in the fifties most Australian women married. Single women, or spinsters as they were disparagingly referred to then, weren't all that common. Remember Colette was supposedly twenty-three when I was born, so it's likely she married within five years of my birth. Most women married by their mid-twenties in those days. However, we need to cross our fingers that she married in New South Wales. If she didn't we've got a real problem. We'll have to chase her through the records of each individual state, and that could take forever. Remember there's no coordinated national register.'

I waited for Margaret's response. Her silence indicated that she knew full well that obtaining Colette's marriage certificate, provided such a document did in fact exist, was indeed the logical next step. Nonetheless, she wasn't going to encourage me to break the law. Frankly, I didn't worry about breaking the law again. I was prepared to do anything necessary to find the woman I was after.

After my initial encounter with the Registry of Births, Deaths and Marriages in Sydney, I dreaded the thought of returning. I didn't want to go through that process again. So I phoned, learning to my relief that I could apply in writing for a five-year marriage search and thus avoid having to attend in person. If Colette had in fact married in New South Wales within five years of my birth, conceivably I would have the certificate within two weeks if luck went my way.

Because I felt so paranoid about applying illegally yet again, I typed a letter using Margaret's Melbourne address, signing it in the name of Paul Darcy — the name Colette had given me at birth — before posting it off to Sydney. To avoid compromising Margaret in any way, I didn't mention what I proposed to do before mailing the letter. In the event, Margaret couldn't have cared less. She understood what needed to be done.

The next few weeks dragged unbearably as I waited for a reply. Although we'd been after Colette for six months now, I kept reassuring myself that it really wasn't all that long. Some people spent years searching, only to draw a total blank. That was the outcome I feared more than anything.

Out of the blue, Margaret phone me in the office one morning, her voice choked with excitement. 'Gordon, I've got it, I've got it, I've got the certificate, and I'm absolutely positive it's your mother's! However, guess what? You won't believe this. I don't think you're Aboriginal!'

'What on earth are you talking about?' I stammered, as the import of what Margaret was saying sunk in. 'Say that again. Tell me slowly. Start at the beginning and tell me everything, absolutely everything. I want to know every tiny detail!'

'Well, the certificate states that Colette Darcy married a planter's son born in Colombo, Sri Lanka. He has to be your father! It's so obvious, don't you think! She didn't marry an Anglo-Saxon.' I felt my identity crumbling there and then.

Uncomfortable about discussing personal matters on office phones at the best of times, I slipped out of the Department and raced home to continue the conversation. Seconds after arriving, I was back on the phone to Margaret.

'What's on the certificate? What does it say?' I pleaded.

'Well, Colette's occupation is listed as "record buyer". She was twenty-six when she married a Sri Lankan named Vivian Edmund Gunesekara. According to the certificate, he was a student, the son of a planter. Colette and Vivian were married in central Sydney, at St Barnabas' Church of England on Broadway. Colette's mother Moira is listed as a witness to the wedding. However, it's the other witness that really interests me. He could prove the key to finding Colette. His name is John Radic; there can't be many of them. I'll check the Sydney phone directory and see what I come up with. With a bit of luck he'll still be living in Sydney.'

As always, Margaret proved right on target. Quickly finding the Radics, she could hardly wait to phone. Margaret had no doubt we were on to a sure thing.

'But what on earth will you tell him?' I queried. 'Surely he'll be suspicious.'

'Don't worry,' replied Margaret. 'I don't see any real problem. Presumably John Radic is married. I'll phone during the day when he'll be at work and hope I catch his wife at home alone. That'd be better. It's always easier to talk to women.'

'But what exactly are you going to say?' I couldn't imagine how Margaret would approach things.

'Oh, I'll just say that I'm aware they were friends of Colette and Vivian's and that now I wish to renew contact myself. Would they be able to assist?'

I couldn't believe Margaret's gall. I wouldn't have had the guts to do anything like what she was planning. She never ceased to amaze me. 'Ring me as soon as you know anything,' I instructed.

'Don't worry,' replied Margaret. 'I promise I'll call them today and get back to you some time tonight.'

I pounced on the phone the instant it rang soon after my return home from work. It was Margaret on the line.

'I've got them, I've got them! I found out everything,' declared Margaret triumphantly. 'The wife was lovely; couldn't have been more pleasant and entirely unsuspicious.'

'But what did she say?'

'She told me that they had indeed been good friends, especially Vivian and her husband John, a veterinary surgeon. The Radics received Christmas cards from Colette and Vivian for a while, but hadn't heard from them in recent years. Mrs Radic thought that unless they'd moved again — wait for this — they'd still be resident in the United States. When the Radics last heard, Vivian — who by the way is a scientist — was involved in research work at Iowa State University. The university's located in a town called Ames. Have you heard of it?' Basically I knew nothing about Iowa: corn and cowboys, virtually nothing else.

'Let's talk later,' I suggested excitedly. 'I'm going to try and find out more.'

While I'd been searching for Colette, I had also been looking for a public administration course at a US Ivy League university. I was applying for scholarships in an effort to raise the money to start the following year. Conscious of the government's historically paternalistic attitude towards Aboriginals, I had little doubt that as Australia's first diplomatic officer of Aboriginal descent recruited through regular channels, I would obtain funds somewhere in the bureaucracy. I had already been recommended for a Fulbright scholarship. My interest in selecting a university with a suitable course had led me to the Australian–American Educational Foundation in Canberra where copies of handbooks for US educational institutions were held. I visited quite frequently.

Hanging up from Margaret, I jumped into the car and headed for the Foundation. Scanning the shelves, I quickly discovered the handbook I required, seconds later the relevant listing: Vivian Edmund Gunesekara, Associate Professor, Department of Biochemistry and Biophysics.

The next step was obvious. Returning home, I dialled the international operator to obtain a residential address and home telephone number in Ames. I was certain there wouldn't be too many Sri Lankans with tongue-twister Sinhalese surnames resident in Ames, Iowa. A few minutes later, the operator provided me with the phone number and address. Colette and Vivian were now firmly in my grasp.

Margaret and I spoke shortly afterwards, to plot our final strategy. 'Well, I suppose you want me to phone?' asked Margaret in a tone demanding an affirmative reply.

For an instant I faltered, realising the magnitude of what was now so terrifyingly imminent. We had almost reached the end of the rainbow. 'We still don't know conclusively if we've got the right woman,' I reassured myself, despite the absurdity of the idea.

'Remember, there's a thirteen-hour time difference,' I warned Margaret.

'No problem,' she said excitedly, as eager as I was for our

shared saga to reach its finale. 'I'll stay up to phone. I want to try and catch Colette late morning her time. She's most likely to be alone in the house then.'

'But how are you going to approach the call? What are you going to say?'

'I always use the same approach; it's quite simple really. To start with, I'll tell Colette who I am and mention that I'm calling from Melbourne. Usually I claim to work within the adoption triangle or something like that. The essential thing is to introduce the word adoption into the conversation as early as possible. That way, the mothers know exactly what's coming. They've been warned. You really don't need to tell them anything after that. They know instinctively.'

'Call me during the night no matter what if you find something out, won't you?' I urged. 'Don't worry about the time.'

That night I went to bed wracked with fear, my mind chaotic as I imagined a myriad outcomes. Tossing around, I lapsed into disturbed sleep until around midnight when I awoke abruptly to the phone ringing. Pulling myself together, I stumbled out of bed and careered blindly down the passageway in search of the receiver. Raising it, I heard Margaret's faint sobbing on the other end.

'It is your mother, and she did marry your father. They have three other children apart from you, a girl and two boys. The girl's the eldest. She's twenty-nine. Your youngest brother is twenty-one, the other one, twenty-five. Your mother knew instantly what I was calling about. She was delighted beyond words. Says it's all her dreams come true. She was going to phone Vivian at the university to tell him. They're going to call you tonight,' continued Margaret, excited and emotional, barely pausing to draw breath. Stunned, I sank into a chair.

'But tell me everything. Every single word. I want to know all of it.'

'Colette answered; it was late-morning, a cold winter's day.

Later in the conversation she told me that snow was tumbling down. "Hello," I said. "My name is Margaret Campi, I'm calling from Melbourne, Australia. Could I please speak to Colette Gunesekara?" "Yes, speaking," Colette replied, surprise in her voice. I could sense her wondering, who on earth can this be? "I work for the adoption triangle." "Yes." There was a long pause until finally she murmured. "Is this about the 21st of June 1952?" "Yes," I answered. "I've waited a long time for this call," said Colette softly.

'Colette told me that the timing of my call had been uncanny. She'd been psychosomatically ill the week before and still wasn't well. She and Vivian returned less that two weeks ago from a trip to Europe. Travelling in Italy, Colette had purposely selected one particular tour because she knew it would include people from Melbourne. She even carried photos of the three children to show people on the off chance that someone might say, ah … I know someone who looks like that! Of course no one ever did, and depression struck when she returned to the States.

'You know she's never stopped thinking about you. Said she'd prayed constantly for this to happen. Incredible that my call should have come at a time when she was suffering so intensely. She and Vivian'll call you tonight when you return from work.'

I didn't return directly to bed. My mind disordered, I paced the living room, half listening to music and tossing back whiskies. Eventually I prepared to head for the bedroom for a few hours' sleep. It was going to be a busy day at work so a sickie was out of the question.

As I flicked the living room light switch, the phone rang. Stunned, I had no idea what to do. I couldn't deal with this right now. I knew precisely who the caller would be. Forcing myself to the phone, I raised the receiver, recognising instantly the international dial tone. For a moment no one spoke until finally a well-spoken female voice enquired, 'May I speak to Gordon Matthews?'

'Yes, speaking,' I replied falteringly before stopping dead. I couldn't bring myself to utter a single word more.

'Do you know who this is?'

'Yes, I know who it is,' I managed to whisper. A pause hung in the air. Then it shattered.

'Please forgive me, please forgive me. You must forgive me for what I did but I had no choice.' Within thirty seconds of speaking to my mother for the first time she was crying.

'I know you couldn't keep your baby,' I managed to blurt out, my voice cracking as tears welled inside. The thought of Colette's unimaginable loss and the grief she had carried since was too hideous for me to deal with.

'You must forgive me,' continued Colette, struggling to speak.

'I know you couldn't keep your baby,' I repeated. 'I never thought otherwise. You don't have to explain anything to me. You must understand. I know that no single woman who fell pregnant in those days could keep her child. The system didn't allow for that. I feel your loss. It took enormous courage to do what you did. I have always thought of your sacrifice as the most selfless thing anyone did for me.'

I meant that from the bottom of my heart. What society had inflicted on her was savage beyond words. For more than thirty years she had suffered a gaping wound inside. At that precise moment I felt I would have killed anyone who harmed her again. I couldn't begin to contemplate the extent of her grief; to tackle and resolve it there and then with organised thought.

Colette was desperate to hear absolutely everything about me. We talked about my father and how excited he would be, and about their other children, my new brothers and sister, and about the thirty-four years Colette had grieved silently wondering where and how I was.

CHAPTER 20

Missing Pieces

Soon after I arrived home from work the next day, Colette and Vivian phoned and I spoke to my father for the first time. I was entranced, totally mesmerised, like a child with a new toy.

Vivian's race and colour had been the defining mystery of my life and now those missing pieces of myself were finally being revealed. My fascination was insatiable; I hung on every word of his softly spoken, heavily accented English. Over the following weeks we phoned each other constantly, both hungry for the tiniest details of each other's lives.

I also spoke frequently to Colette who reminded me several times that she had never wanted to give me away, mentioning how three months after my birth she had contacted Auntie Rose in search of a photo. Auntie Rose had conveyed Colette's request to Mum and Dad who, after careful consideration, declined to oblige on the basis that a photo would not help Colette adjust to her circumstances and accept the decision that she had made, their position unsurprising for the times. In those days, both parties were informed that the identification of adoptees would never be divulged. This must have caused enormous pain for relinquishing mothers. Assuming the ground rules wouldn't change, some adoptive parents never told their children that they were adopted, secure in the belief that the law would protect their decision to remain silent.

Colette also explained tearfully that before one of only three return trips she had made to Australia in more than thirty years, a name and Melbourne address which she believed might be mine had appeared in a dream. Arriving at Sydney Airport, Colette had unsuccessfully consulted a Melbourne telephone directory before dejectedly leaving the terminal. Due to her absence in the United States, Colette had also been unaware of the changes to Victorian state adoption legislation and the existence of a register on which she was qualified to place her name to indicate she wished to contact her relinquished child.

Although Colette and Vivian had never told anyone about my birth, understandably they now wanted to tell their other children as soon as possible. Only Mark, my twenty-one-year-old youngest brother, still lived at home. Janet, my sister, had a high-powered corporate job and lived in Houston, Texas. Steven, the elder of my two new brothers, lived in Chicago, also working for a major corporation. Both travelled extensively with work, returning home infrequently. Nowadays, the family was only together twice a year: Christmas and Thanksgiving.

By chance, Thanksgiving happened to be around the corner, only a few weeks away. To ease their burden, Colette and Vivian were keen to use the opportunity to explain to the children what had happened more than thirty years before in Australia. I understood their need but my own feelings were radically different.

For my part, I was plagued with anxiety and confusion, now knowing that I was of Sri Lankan and not Aboriginal descent. The instant Margaret first explained the contents of Colette's marriage

certificate, my world had begun to unravel. Undoubtedly it was
the most devastating news I had ever received, tearing the rug out
from under my feet. For a decade and a half I had claimed to be
something that I was not. Margaret's news, conveyed in a few
shattering seconds, had redefined entirely the parameters of who
I was. Now I felt fraudulent and uncertain as to what I might do. I
was also terrified that someone might find out. Apart from my
adoptive mother, Kay and one close friend, no one else had the
vaguest idea about anything that had transpired.

The fact that Vivian was Sri Lankan and not Aboriginal struck
me as steeped in irony. My conviction ever since childhood that
my natural father wasn't white had now been confirmed as
entirely correct but my belief that he was Aboriginal had been
proved wrong. Moreover, although it remained uncertain when
and from where Aboriginal people arrived in Australia, one theory
advanced by anthropologists suggests that they arrived from
South Asia, of which Sri Lanka and India both form a part.

Although I dreaded telling Colette and Vivian about my mistaken identity, I longed to speak to them before they spoke to the
children. Reluctantly I broached the subject.

'There's something important I need to talk to you about,' I
ventured.

Both were understandably curious. 'Of course, Gordon. What
is it?'

'Well, perhaps it's not really that important. Nothing to worry
about. It's just that we need to talk, but I'd prefer to do it in person
rather than over the phone. Would you mind if I came to visit? I'd
like to do that.'

The response I anticipated arrived instantly. 'You're welcome in
this house any time you care to come. You know that. Now it's
your home too.'

'I'll have to see if I can organise things at work so I'm able to take holidays soon. I'll try to make it over within the next few months.'

'But what is there that's so special you can't tell us about it now? You can talk to us about anything. We hope you understand that. Absolutely anything.'

'Don't worry. There's nothing to worry about. I'll explain everything when we meet.'

Colette and Vivian were insistent about not delaying unnecessarily and telling their children during Thanksgiving. Vivian even wrote to me stressing how important it was for them to break the news as soon as possible. Reluctantly I agreed.

Colette and I spoke daily in the lead-up to Thanksgiving. She was apprehensive about what she and Vivian faced though quite clear about what had to be done. How I ached to speak to Colette and Vivian about my problem. My Aboriginality was going to affect our eventual reunion and they needed to hear about it as soon as possible. Then they would understand exactly how I'd come to reappear in their lives.

With Thanksgiving Day imminent, I could barely contain myself as I contemplated how it would unfold. When Colette finally phoned, she sounded incredibly relieved; everything appeared to have gone as well as could be expected. My natural mother explained how she and Vivian had approached things in as calm a manner as possible.

In terms of the mechanics of the event, Naomi, Steven's girlfriend, had represented the only complication. Unexpectedly, at the last minute, Naomi had decided to celebrate the holiday with the Gunesekaras rather than with her own family. While careful not to say anything to the children prior to Thanksgiving Day itself, Colette had mentioned to Steven that there was something important that she and Vivian needed to discuss privately, subtly suggesting that Naomi's presence might complicate things somewhat. Steven insisted on bringing Naomi along. She had her heart set firmly on the visit. 'Don't worry Mum,' Steven had reassured. 'I'll send her off for a stroll when it's time for us to talk.'

Following a long leisurely lunch, the family retired to the television room while Naomi took her walk. She would return in an hour. The family settled quickly, the children listening dumbfounded as Colette and Vivian explained my existence and what had happened all those years ago in Australia. Despite the shock, all three children appeared to take the news well. Steven had feared something worse: that Colette or Vivian had cancer or some other terminal illness, something devastating like that.

Colette was full of praise for her sons. They had opened their hearts generously. 'When I told Steven, he looked at me with such sorrow and compassion. All that mattered to him was that what was happening was what I really wanted. "This guy turning up's not gonna bother you, is it?" he asked. "This is definitely something you wanted?" "Oh yes," I replied as he stroked me gently. I really couldn't have wished for anything more. Likewise, Mark's reaction was one of total acceptance. I'm just so proud. The boys have been absolutely wonderful,' sighed Colette contentedly.

Colette was slightly more circumspect when it came to Janet's reaction. 'Janet really didn't say much at all,' confided Colette. 'I was quite surprised. In fact, I thought they'd all have far more questions than they actually did. I guess they were all in shock. Janet withdrew upstairs to her bedroom. I suppose she wanted to contemplate privately what we told her.'

Janet's retreat to her room did in fact signify that all was not well. Her behaviour changed dramatically the following day. Irritable, Janet lashed out at Vivian, the focus of her anger. When he tried to discuss things, she yelled at him to get out of her room. The next day she went one step further, ignoring him altogether and behaving as if he didn't exist.

Although disappointed, Colette accepted it stoically, hopeful that things would eventually settle down. 'I'm sure Janet will come around. She probably just needs a day or two to recover from the shock. Anyhow, I can only worry so much. What has happened is just the most wonderful thing for me, what I wanted to happen more than anything else in my life. At the end of the day, if the children can't share my joy and come along for the ride, then that's just too bad. I've devoted my life to them and now it's my turn. I pray they'll understand what I've been through and understand the joy I'm feeling now, although if things don't turn out that way, I can live with that too. This is a very difficult time for everyone and each of us is going to react differently.'

Over the ensuing weeks, Colette wrote almost daily. I got used to going to the letterbox knowing I'd find something. However, the first letter she wrote the day after we spoke initially — the most important letter of my life — never arrived. We both felt extremely uncomfortable about it. Colette checked repeatedly with the post office in Ames while I did the same thing in Canberra. However, our efforts proved fruitless. No one could shed any light on the missing letter; it had simply vanished.

The thought of a stranger reading the letter horrified me beyond words, especially someone living in my apartment block who might identify me. After all, other departmental employees shared the same address. Nothing ever arrived though, and in time we gave up hope of the letter ever appearing, Colette berating herself for not having kept a copy.

On Christmas Eve, just before heading down to Melbourne to spend Christmas with the family, I checked the letterbox one last time. My heart skipped a beat. Inside lay a tatty, rain-stained aerogram. Picking it up, I noticed instantly that the letter had been opened and resealed with cellotape. Trembling, I slowly pulled it open. Inside the aerogram was an unsigned note which read:

Mr Matthews, words cannot describe my guilt at having read this letter. However, I found it lying wet and discarded in the street. I hope it finds the right person this time.

Pushing the note aside I devoured Colette's letter.

6 November 1986

Dear Gordon,

Two dates will always be seared in my brain. 21 June and 5 November. I am sure Margaret told you of my reactions, and you also must have been experiencing many, many emotions. I called Vivian immediately, and the first time he was not able to say very much. People were in his office, and the next time I spoke to him he told me he had prayed every night for that phone call.

That evening when he came home, he asked me to repeat everything. He wept, and I'm sure you could tell by his voice when he initially spoke to you, how much emotion he was feeling. Even the timing of Margaret's call was incredible. I was in the kitchen, where I answered the phone. Mark and his girlfriend had gone into the family room about 15 minutes earlier, and so I was free to talk. I felt Margaret's kindness and support over the phone, and would you please thank her for that.

I still feel in a state of shock. Your maturity, understanding and straight-forwardness impressed me tremendously, and I knew I was speaking to a very special, rare person. What you said later confirmed it, but I knew immediately you had been raised by a very special woman, and that mother loved you enough to say 'find your birth parents'. My heart knows no way to express the gratitude I feel.

You asked that I not tell Janet, Steven and Mark immediately, as you had something you wanted to tell me first. I shall wait to hear from you how you would like things to be handled. Mark still lives at home, and Janet and Steven will be here for Thanksgiving on 27 November, the 23rd being her birthday, and Steven probably just for a couple of days. They both have very demanding jobs, and it is sometimes very difficult for them to all be home at the same time. What is really running through my mind is, wouldn't it be better to tell them when we are together and can talk? I know they will get a shock and will have many, many questions.

It is incredible that you have been so close by in Ohio, and we used to live quite close to Columbus. Hardly a day went by that I didn't wonder where you were, how you were … questions, questions. Even the trip to Europe bothered me, there were people from Melbourne on our tour, and I was always wondering if by some strange coincidence they knew you. So many times I even thought you might be visiting Ames, and everywhere I went looked for a face that might show a family resemblance. To answer your question about coming to the US, do what is best for you. Janet will be in Hawaii from 6 to 15 February with a girlfriend, and she had wanted us to come to Houston soon after. But that can always be rearranged. Vivian has some meetings in Geneva, New York, for a few days, but as yet does not have a date. It will be some time in March.

I'm sure you know we could have very bad weather the months you mentioned, although last year the winter was relatively mild. It is all so incredible you can make this trip. Is it a combined business trip? You have done so much, and accomplished so much, it is amazing. I am hungry to hear more.

Your family in Australia must be going through a very emotional time also, not just Vivian and myself. Do your brother and sisters know you found us? I never ever told anyone about your birth, and only shared the terrible sense of loss I have carried with Vivian. I only pray that Janet, Steven and Mark will be as loving and understanding as you, and then I will know I have been truly blessed.

My love and prayers for you are in this letter.

Colette

PS Because of my part-time job, I get lots of phone calls, so feel free to call. If Mark is present and I can't talk, you will know by my manner immediately. Do you have a photograph? I'll let you know if there are family resemblances.

CHAPTER 21

An Aboriginal Son

Three months after finding Colette and Vivian, I finally embarked on the trip of my life. At thirty-four, I was off to meet new parents in the United States. Despite my joy, I dreaded the thought of having to explain the extraordinary confusion surrounding my race and its unforeseen consequences.

So obsessively paranoid was I about my situation that only my mother in Melbourne, my sister Kay and one friend knew what I was doing. Officially I was still Aboriginal with obligations and now I knew I wasn't. I'd been wrong. Everyone at work considered me bonkers, sacrificing an Australian summer to holiday in a freezing North American winter.

A week or so before leaving Australia, I visited Mum in Melbourne. We discussed my forthcoming visit. 'What do you think I could send Colette and Vivian?' she asked, out of the blue. 'I'm not sure what would be appropriate, but I'd like to send them something.' Mum's comment made me uncomfortable. How did I reply to that? I wondered what she really thought about what I was doing. Deep inside was she saddened by it all? Was I stabbing at her heart? I honestly didn't think so. Mum was bigger than all that, she knew what was important. 'No one owns anyone in this life,' she used to say. Yet I felt the same sense of guilt and betrayal I had when I first began searching. I'd had a family for more than thirty years, now I was off to meet another I'd discovered barely three months before.

'Don't worry Mum, you really don't have to send them anything. They won't be expecting a thing. You couldn't have been any more supportive and now I'm actually going. Just think, after waiting thirty-four years they're finally going to meet their first child. Imagine how excited they must be. I'm sure that's more than enough as far as they're concerned,' I told her, desperate to appear nonchalant while secretly dying inside. I prayed that Mum wasn't too hurt by what I was doing.

Although I'd assumed that was the end of Mum's idea, I was mistaken. Just before heading back to Canberra, she handed me an envelope. 'I've written you a note. Read it when you want although maybe you should wait until you begin your trip. There's also a short letter I'd like you to give to Colette and Vivian. I've left it open for you to read if you like.' Embarrassed by Mum's gesture I thanked her and tucked the small envelope away.

I completely forgot about the note until just after my Air Canada flight departed Sydney, the aircraft soaring upwards as Botany Bay trailed away below. Pulling the envelope out of the inside pocket where I'd placed it for safe keeping, I opened it hesitantly. Clearly it contained something special. Mum always came up with simple but beautiful words on important occasions. She had a special gift for things like that.

The first note was for me:

Dearest Gordon,

Please give the enclosed note to Colette and Vivian. I have left it open for you to read.

May courage, integrity and lots and lots of my love go with you on this special journey.

Safe return.

Mum

Mum's note to Colette and Vivian read:

My dear Colette and Vivian,

Enclosed is one of my favourite photographs of Gordon as a baby, with a curl from his first haircut.

My gratitude to you both for the privilege of Rodney and I being an integral part of Gordon's life is very great indeed.

He is a son to be proud of and to love very dearly.

Now I feel sure you both will help him reach his full potential.

Yours with love,

Bell Matthews

My throat ached as I struggled to hold back tears.
In Montreal, I spent a few days with friends, all of whom found

me inexplicably uptight. None of them had any idea of the real purpose of my trip until, the night before flying to Iowa, I downed copious beers in a bar with one particular mate. Soon the alcohol had its effect.

'You're in a really strange mood, Gordon. What's up?' he enquired.

'I don't want to talk about it,' I answered defensively. Sensing that something unusual was afoot, my friend continued to prod.

'I'm adopted and tomorrow I've got the most important day of my life,' I replied eventually to shut him up. No further explanation was needed. Now, understanding what was gnawing at me, my friend eased off.

Later that night, Colette and I spoke on the phone for what would be our final conversation prior to meeting. Our exchange was intimate and warm, Colette's happiness evident as she readied herself for our big day. I felt delighted for my natural mother. The next day she would be meeting her firstborn whom she had never wished to surrender and about whose life she had only been able to guess for more than three decades. I couldn't begin to imagine how that might feel. I recalled Colette commenting once about how difficult Christmas and birthdays had been following my adoption, my natural mother revealing how she and Vivian would cry themselves to sleep, overcome by despair. I pictured Colette and Vivian weeping together, muffling their sorrow lest one of the children should hear.

Leaving Montreal the following afternoon, the city looked bleak and shrouded in grey. The journey to Iowa would take three-and-a-half hours — considerably shorter than I would have liked. The reality of what was terrifyingly imminent overwhelmed me completely.

Montreal to Chicago was the first stage of the journey, an hour-long flight; in Chicago, I swapped aircraft for the onward journey to Iowa. Transit time was barely thirty minutes and I desperately wished it were longer. While I had fantasised all my life about such a journey, the reality of what was unfolding undermined my courage. Terrified of losing control, I ached to postpone the meeting. I imagined myself shredded layer by layer and created anew.

Pacing restlessly around the departure lounge, a young Canadian strolled up unexpectedly and began to chat. 'So, you're off to Des Moines. An Australian headed for Des Moines. What on earth are you going there for?'

'Oh, I know some people,' I replied, suppressing the unease his arrival aroused. This conversation was the last thing I needed. 'I'll be staying with them for several weeks,' I added matter-of-factly.

The Canadian, a computer programmer, lived in Des Moines. I could hardly believe it. 'Just my luck,' I bemoaned privately, fearful that I had acquired an undesired travel companion.

'Listen, I've got friends who are meeting me at the airport. If no one's picking you up, they could give you a lift to wherever it is you're going. I'm sure they wouldn't mind. It'll be freezing in Des Moines when we arrive, snow everywhere.'

'I'm actually not staying in Des Moines. I'm heading for Ames and I'm being met,' I responded. 'But thanks anyway.'

I wished the guy would just evaporate. The possibility that he might intrude when we arrived horrified me. The last thing I needed on first meeting Colette and Vivian was a stray acquaintance to introduce. Eventually I withdrew to the rest room. Every second alone was crucial. I needed to prepare for what was about to occur.

Fortunately the flight wasn't full. I settled in a vacant row cradling a bottle of duty-free whisky which I had anticipated might prove handy. What better than a few charges to suppress my creeping anxiety. Tucked away in the rear smoking section, I glanced around in search of the Canadian who, to my relief, I sighted much further down the aircraft.

This final leg was a short one, around an hour and a half. An irrepressible desire to escape overwhelmed me. Desperate to focus on something else, my eyes roamed the cabin in search of distractions. Flight attendants cruised lazily up and down the aisle, offering soft drinks and the packets of nuts that US airlines routinely serve in economy class. Gulping my drink, I replaced it with a generous whisky. Time now was hideously short. Never had I felt so on edge.

As the plane started its descent, all I could think about was escape. I imagined vanishing silently down the toilet chute or something like that, disappearing untraceably into the night. As my fear mounted, the lights of the city appeared below. Suddenly I could make out the airport, then the silhouette of the terminal, its lights dancing across the tarmac. It was difficult to believe they were waiting inside, these people I had never met. The parents I had never known.

Now escape was impossible. My sense of self began to disintegrate. I was about to be changed irrevocably and I knew it. No way to reverse the aircraft and thrust upwards again into the wintry night. Finally I was about to find out where I had come from; to meet the two individuals who had given me life.

The plane taxied in, deep banks of snow lining the tarmac. Mercifully, I was seated about three-quarters of the way down the aircraft. As the other passengers disembarked, I dallied as long as possible; slipping on my jacket, adjusting my scarf, fiddling with the hand luggage, postponing the inevitable until it became unavoidable. My rehearsals seemed irrelevant now. This was the real thing.

Marching along the tunnel from the aircraft to the terminal, I imagined myself walking the gangplank. Myriad thoughts whirled frantically inside my head. Was I going to recognise them? Would they recognise me? What were we going to say? Would things unfold smoothly? That walk was the longest of my life, my stomach churning sickeningly.

Unlike me, Colette and Vivian knew who they were looking for. They had already seen me. At Colette's request, I had forwarded two photographs of myself: one taken two years before with Brazilian children in a Rio de Janeiro *favela*; the other, a Melbourne Cup celebration in the Department just a few days before I had first spoken to Colette. To foster cup spirit, the party theme had been hats. Never having owned a hat, I had borrowed a Mexican sombrero which swam ridiculously over my head. It didn't bother me that I looked absurd.

For my part, I had no firm idea how Colette and Vivian looked; their faces were still sources of fantasy to me. That was exactly how I'd wanted it. I preferred to meet them in person with as few preconceptions as possible.

My incomplete notion of how my natural parents looked was based on titbits of information gleaned here and there. Basically all I knew was that Colette was white while Vivian was not, and that both were relatively short. In an initial conversation, Colette and Vivian had mentioned that they were both around five feet six inches, in stark contrast with their taller offspring. During our conversation the previous evening, Colette had told me that she would wear a mauve-coloured coat to help me identify her and that she and Vivian would stand quietly at the back of the arrival hall. Our meeting was going to be low key. That suited me fine.

Emerging from the tunnel, I encountered a sea of faces. The terminal literally throbbed with activity. Staring towards the rear of the crowd, I expected to spot Colette and Vivian instantly. They were nowhere to be seen.

Contrary to Colette's advice, the two of them waited much

closer to the gate. Although I completely missed them, they honed in on me. A woman approached. Suddenly I realised who it was. Our eyes met. Colette smiled warmly.

'Gordon?'

'Yes, that's right, that's me,' I responded lamely, uncertain what to say next.

My first impression was of how dissimilar we looked. It was not until much later that I could begin to see myself in either of them. It occurred to me that had I bumped into Colette unwittingly, never in a million years would I have imagined that this woman was in fact my birth mother.

Sporting a tweed jacket, tailored trousers and peaked beret, Vivian exuded discipline and moderation; the influence of his British-style education plainly evident. His appearance gave an impression of orderliness which I would be reminded of throughout my stay whenever he approached a meal or prepared the fruit he consumed daily. Everything was dealt with methodically and thoroughly. By the end of my visit I would find it impossible to imagine Vivian being less than fully diligent in relation to anything. I was also fascinated to see first-hand his skin colour, the rich deep brown I had anticipated.

Slim and slight in stature, Colette radiated warmth, softness and timidity. Like her husband, my natural mother's appearance was groomed and unpretentious. Her blouse was simple, she wore plain jewellery. I could imagine her wearing a string of pearls on a special occasion. A tidy and compact couple, Colette and Vivian appeared to complement each other perfectly.

We kissed and exchanged greetings, chatting superficially for several minutes within the anonymity of the crowd. While hardly the most intimate setting, it struck me that introducing ourselves this way was less pressured than if the three of us had met alone. In view of the enormity of the event, there was something absurdly inadequate, vaguely banal, about our encounter. I thought involuntarily of Livingstone and Stanley. Each of us was slightly awkward in our new roles as family members.

Eventually we moved on to the baggage collection area. My Canadian acquaintance glanced over at my 'friends', a perplexed look on his face. I wondered whether or not Colette and Vivian matched his image of whom I might possibly be visiting in Ames. Did he assume they were my parents? For a moment I sensed he was about to stroll over. Thankfully, he remained at bay.

At that precise moment, I felt myself clinging to my established identity before it disintegrated forever. The fact that I had now met my natural parents compelled me to redefine myself completely. In a way I felt as if I'd been shaped anew. Something had changed within me. I was a different person now.

During our phone conversation the previous night, Colette had warned she wouldn't be able to keep her eyes away from me. I recalled her words later; she meant precisely what she had said. Seated in the back seat as we journeyed towards my new 'home', Colette turned repeatedly to face me from the front. Chatting disjointedly, we rambled from subject to subject, my visit to Montreal, the economic situation in Australia, work in the Department, then on to yet another relative I'd never heard of — a Sri Lankan engineer resident in Montreal who was one of Vivian's favourite uncles.

Then Colette said, 'By the way, we've been dying to know what it was you wanted to talk about,' and my heart skipped a beat. My Aboriginal problem had surfaced confrontingly even earlier than I had anticipated. How was I going to deal with it? I couldn't begin to imagine.

'Oh, it's nothing special. Why don't we talk about it later?' I suggested, downplaying the question, trying to sound as casual as possible. 'It really isn't that important.'

Moving further into the night along a freeway laden with snow, my thoughts settled on our ultimate destination and imminent

arrival. My mind returned to November and the one extraordinary week in which I solved the mystery of my race and
discovered new parents and three American siblings on the other
side of the world. It seemed ludicrous that now, as a direct result
of my racial problem, I found myself driving through rural Iowa,
preparing to explain to my natural parents the story of their
'Aboriginal son'. I couldn't imagine anything more bizarre.

An hour or so later we arrived. Pulling into the drive, my
younger brother emerged unexpectedly to assist with the luggage, catching me completely off guard. I'd primed myself to meet
him inside. An icy wind soughed eerily through the trees. It was
impossible to discern anything of my surroundings in the dark.

'How ya doin' Gordon?' greeted Mark shyly.

'I'm well Mark, how are you? Great to meet you,' I replied
nervously, the two of us observing one another under an indif-
ferent moon.

The first thing that struck me about Mark was his physique.
More solid than me, Mark was overweight, more so than I had
been at his age. I was transfixed though by his face. For the very
first time I could recognise myself in another person's face. For an
adopted person, that was an indescribable feeling.

Hurrying inside to escape the cold, the four of us settled in the
family room. Despite Colette's absence from Australia for the
major part of her life, the room featured distinctively Australian
touches. Framed mimi-figure prints and watercolours by Namat-
jira and other mission artists hung above an open brick fireplace.
A hand-painted ceramic plate decorated with a garish portrait of a
tribal Aboriginal stared down from above the sideboard beside
lithographs of Australian wildflowers and framed prints of Aboriginal bark paintings. A boomerang purchased by Vivian from
Aboriginals on the Nullarbor during the journey from Perth to

Melbourne immediately following his arrival in Australia completed the collage.

Colette fussed around, offering tea and snacks. While she was in the kitchen out of hearing range, Mark leant towards me conspiratorially. 'You know Mum's spent weeks preparing for your visit, scrubbing everything with a vengeance. The fridge is groanin', man — worse than at Christmas. She's just so happy to have you here.' The two of us chuckled like old buddies.

When Mark eventually dragged himself off to bed, I found myself alone with Colette and Vivian for the first time. 'Why don't you two guys give each other a hug?' suggested Colette. 'You haven't had a chance yet.' Father and son embraced self-consciously, while Colette watched contentedly. Vivian was shy, clearly not someone who revealed his emotions easily. Unfortunately, I had inherited that aspect of his personality. I had to keep reminding myself that this slight, reserved Sri Lankan man I held in my arms was in fact my father. The three of us were at a loss as to what to do next. I suggested we look at the family photos I had brought with me. In retrospect, my suggestion was ridiculously premature.

Baby photos, primary school snaps, a silly eisteddfod shot of me as an English parson, several Christmas photographs snapped by Dad beneath the silver birch which dominated our front garden, summer holidays at Anglesea with Pop and Gran Brodrick, the picnic blanket laden with goodies beside our Austin. As we progressed through them, Colette clasped Vivian's hand and sobbed silently as my formative years with the family that had raised me unfolded in steady succession before her.

After talking some more, we retired upstairs where Colette and Vivian showed me to my bedroom. My brother Steven's room, it was the sort of bedroom the majority of my friends had grown up in. This room might have been mine under different circumstances. Unpacking my suitcase, I pondered how different life would have been here in Iowa, a world away from Australia and East Kew.

Glancing down at the pillow, I was taken aback. Positioned in the centre was a key on a leather and gold ring, a housekey. Fondling the ring, which featured my first initial, the significance of my visit for Colette and Vivian struck home. Not only was this the most important day of my life, clearly it was the same for them. Their firstborn child had come home.

Before going to bed, I went to Colette and Vivian's bedroom to give them Bell's envelope. Glancing through the door, I was shocked to see one of the two photos I had sent positioned strategically on the dressing table at the foot of the bed. Framed and solitary, it faced them. Seeing myself on display in the bedroom of people who had been strangers until now somehow seemed strange. How often through the years had they wondered about me as I had about them? They had never stopped, I realised sadly.

Lying in bed riddled with guilt, sleep proved elusive. I dreaded the thought of having to explain my racial problem to Colette and Vivian. They were good and decent people who had never harmed anyone. I'd sensed that the instant we first spoke. Now, I found myself contemplating how they would react when I explained the consequences of my unclear racial background.

I sank into depression. Why we had all suffered so unnecessarily remained inexplicable. Why had Colette been forced to give me away in the first place? What sort of people devised such inhumane rules? Angrily I thought about the adoption system. It seemed absurd that I should be spending my first night with my parents, unable to sleep due to a mistaken racial identity. My only consolation was that the torment would soon be over. The next day Vivian was going to return home for lunch, taking the rest of the day off work so that I could explain what was troubling me so deeply.

I woke early and went downstairs to the family room. Vivian and Mark had already left for the university. Staring out of the television room through frosted, sliding windows, I noticed cardinals, blue jays and grackle competing for grain from a feeder on a nearby maple tree. Despite the carpet of grimy late-winter snow, spring had clearly arrived. Douglas firs, crab apples, cypresses and a flowering dogwood defied the ferocious early morning frost.

Strolling outside, I viewed the house properly for the first time. Two-storey brick American colonial style, it reminded me instantly of those houses Australian kids of my generation grew up with in TV series like 'Leave it to Beaver'. Quintessential middle America. In common with every other house in the street, the obligatory basketball hoop hung over the garage door. Out the back a solitary water-tower guarded the neighbourhood. However, what struck me most were the perfectly manicured lawns, scarcely a blade of grass out of place. It almost looked painted.

Colette studied me closely as I ate breakfast. I was the most important house guest ever to visit and she wanted everything to be just perfect. Alone for the first time and both insatiably curious, the two of us chatted over coffee, captive to whatever it was the other had to say. However, I still felt preoccupied, my thoughts returning constantly to the conversation we would have when Vivian returned from the office. I'd rehearsed the dialogue ad nauseam.

Some time later, Mark returned from morning classes. We devoured sandwiches before heading off to explore the university campus. This was our first opportunity to spend time together and I was looking forward to a break from the homefront already. Although this was only my first day, I felt unbearably pressured.

Incorporating a new family into my life was not going to be easy, I realised.

'What are you going to say if you run into any of your friends?' Colette asked Mark as the two of us prepared to leave. 'I mean you both look so alike. Someone's bound to notice a family resemblance.'

Mark and I glanced across at each other. My younger brother didn't seem fazed by that possibility I was pleased to note. 'Don't worry Mum. If anyone asks, I'll just say Gordon's a cousin visiting from Australia. No one's gonna think twice about that, are they?'

After Mark had introduced me to the campus — his classrooms, the cafeteria and several faculty buildings — both of us felt in need of a charge to lighten things up. We headed for Carol's Candy Box, a bar located on the edge of the campus. A popular haunt frequented by raucous fraternity and sorority kids, Carol's had served Iowa State students since 1919. Crammed with ball sports memorabilia, it reeked of the midwest. Flags, pennants and banners plastered the walls beneath a vermilion, smoke-stained roof featuring art deco squares. Indoor Track Championship and Chicago Bears pennants, Cleveland Browns posters and original publicity shots of former Iowa State sporting heroes were also displayed. There was even an Australian flag.

Carol's was not one of my brother's regular haunts. It certainly wasn't my scene either, although it did score well when it came to freshly roasted popcorn and spicy 'buffalo wings'. Our visit was brief, less than twenty minutes in fact, which only allowed time to down a couple of beers and not much more. Neither of us said much. I glanced over at Mark, wondering how he might react had he any inkling of the nature of my impending conversation with Colette and Vivian.

Not having any more classes that day, Mark accompanied me back to the house for lunch. The meal concluded, Mark settled in the family room in front of the television while I adjourned to the living room with Colette and Vivian. Discernibly curious about what was going on, Mark was tactful enough not to enquire. 'See you later Mark,' I said before heading off, silently rehearsing my tale one final time. My brother grinned encouragingly. Entering the living room, Colette and Vivian seated themselves deliberately, conscious that this was a special event. Now they would learn how the problem of my race had led me from the other side of the world to rural Iowa. I steadied myself to begin.

'Well ... you know, my uncertain racial background always caused a lot of problems for me,' I began, my throat seizing up, the conversation almost grinding to a halt before I coughed the first sentence out. How ridiculous this must sound, I thought. 'I'm obviously not black, but I'm not white either,' I continued hesitantly, gravely stating the obvious without any sense of irony. 'The fact that I never knew my racial background has caused a lot of confusion. I always thought of myself as coloured, of mixed blood, never an Anglo-Saxon with an olive tinge.'

Colette glanced over at Vivian. 'But I thought they'd just think you were ... I don't know, Italian or Greek or something,' replied Colette softly. 'You're olive skinned. You're not all that dark.'

'But they never did and nor did I,' I replied, selecting words with inordinate care. 'It just never happened like that.' The three of us felt extremely uncomfortable as I explained the constant enquiring and taunting which I had faced growing up.

'At least "Abo" wasn't said with malice. It wasn't meant to offend. Not when I was still young and at primary school. It was intended more as a joke. Nevertheless, it used to embarrass the hell out of me. I always dreaded the thought of someone saying something. It would make me cringe inside, especially if one of the family happened to be around. I hated that more than anything. Sometimes Fiona, Kay and Peter would overhear. Looking back, I guess no one really thought seriously about what they were saying or how it might affect me. That wasn't much consolation though, it didn't make things any easier. I was always different because my colour placed me apart. When it came to background and colour, I was always on my own. I knew I came from somewhere distinct from the rest of them. I felt different.'

Colette and Vivian hung on every word as I continued explaining the extraordinary consequences of the gaps in my knowledge about myself: Scotch College experiences; the fact that as I grew older Bell had thought it likely I possessed Aboriginal blood; and how, because I believed I was Aboriginal, I had claimed a racial identity without conclusive proof, unwilling to permit the adoption system to cheat me of my race.

As my explanation continued, I outlined to Colette and Vivian how the identity of their 'Aboriginal' son had been shaped. Explaining to my parents that they had left me to grow up without my race, was a terrible thing to do.

As I'd feared, my tale overwhelmed Colette and Vivian. At first neither of them said anything, until finally Vivian broke the uncomfortable silence. 'What's going to happen if you tell the Department and your Aboriginal friends the truth? Can't you just tell them what's happened to you,' he asked.

'How can I possibly do that?' I replied. 'To begin with, it'll be the end of my career. The Department's never going to accept this. Sure my background's not typically Aboriginal — middle-class Kew, the doctor's son and all that. But the fact remains that I'm the only person to identify as Aboriginal ever recruited into the career stream of Foreign Affairs and that comes with a profile. The bicentennial's just around the corner and I'm sure it's not just pure coincidence that they've placed me in the branch which handles the United Nations. They'll probably want to trot me out in some capacity during 1988. After all, there's hardly anyone else.

Obviously, they haven't actually spelt things out in so many words; the bureaucracy never would. Still, everyone knows how the system operates.

'And what about my Aboriginal friends? How can I let them down? I've tried to help Aboriginal people enter the Department and increase Aboriginal employment levels. I even arranged a successful Aboriginal affairs cultural awareness program repeated several times as part of the diplomatic training course. I've really tried to contribute. My Aboriginal friends will feel so cheated and disappointed.'

'Disappointed maybe, but not cheated,' interjected Vivian sympathetically.

'But did you honestly think you were of Aboriginal descent?' asked Colette despondently.

'Of course I did,' I replied. 'See it through my eyes. What else could I have been? Born in 1952. Middle-class, suburban Australia was almost exclusively white. The only exceptions, at least where I lived, were a few Chinese whose families had penetrated the middle class, some of them descended from goldfield merchants and labourers who arrived last century. There was a smattering of Chinese boys at Scotch.

'As for Aboriginals, how many of them lived in Melbourne's eastern suburbs in the 1950s and 1960s? None, of course. Given my olive complexion and the fact that virtually no coloured immigrants had entered Australia when I was born, what else could I have been other than Aboriginal, even though there were none in middle-class Australia? Essentially there were no alternatives. Remember, I grew up in a middle-class suburb, in a country with an immigration policy designed to impede the entry of people of colour. Those who overcame the bureaucratic barriers were few and far between. People were incredibly racist in their outlook back in those days. "Got a touch of the tarbrush," they sometimes sniggered derisively. Australia was notoriously insular. Still is in heaps of ways.

'As far as I was concerned, being Aboriginal was the only logical explanation for my colour. I mean, what would you have believed in my situation? All I did was claim my race. How many people live without their racial background, for heaven's sake? I needed to feel real, complete.' Colette and Vivian listened dumbfounded.

'That's why I had to find you. I needed to find you to solve my problem. I had to establish the truth about my race. This whole thing had spun out of control.'

Colette glanced at Vivian, then back over at me. 'So that's why you looked for us. It had nothing to do with wanting to find your parents as such. You weren't primarily looking for us. That wasn't your main motivation. You were searching for your race, weren't you? I wonder if you would have contacted us otherwise?' Before I could respond, Colette passed verdict herself. 'Probably not,' she murmured. 'Probably not.'

This was the question I had dreaded more than anything, acutely aware of the pain an honest reply would inflict. Still how could I lie? 'I honestly don't know,' I replied gently. 'I can't say, although it is true that I contacted you at this particular point in time because of the racial problem. Don't you see? I simply had to find you. There was no other way to solve my problem. Whether or not I would have made contact later on I can't honestly say, and I'll never know that now. What I do know is that I'm here because I needed to establish my race and finding you was the only way to achieve that.

'I want you to know, though, that I always wondered about who and where you both were, as far back as I can remember. I sensed you were suffering and that you never wanted to give away your baby. None of those women sacrificed babies because they wanted to. They had no real choice. Those babies were stolen from their mothers, at least morally that is. It's all so blatantly obvious.'

'And to think all this time I thought I was the only one suffering,' groaned Colette, her voice cracking. 'Not for a minute did I ever imagine that anyone else was too. It never occurred to me that you might be aching as well.

'You know,' she continued, 'Rose never enquired about the racial background of my baby. She would have taken it for granted that you'd be white. After all, how many white Australian women were involved with coloured men back in those days? Hardly any at all. I thought about explaining everything at the time, but something inside cautioned me to remain quiet. I knew instinctively that mentioning Vivian's Ceylonese background would have a detrimental effect on what eventually happened to you. I wanted the best for you, to protect you as much as I could. I didn't want to lose my baby,' she sobbed. 'I never dreamt that not explaining everything would cause such problems. You must forgive me. I'm so terribly sorry. I was in such turmoil at the time. I never imagined how this might unfold.'

'I would have done precisely the same thing you did,' I said, struggling not to cry. 'I don't doubt that for a minute. No woman in your position would have mentioned Vivian. Not in Australia in 1952. Never, never, never.'

'Let me tell you something. When I eventually told Auntie Rose a few months back that Vivian was Sri Lankan, she told me that if she had known at the time I was up for adoption, I would have been placed with — hang on, let me get this right … how did she put it? — a more 'accepting' family is the phrase I recall her using. She also said I might have ended up a ward of the state although she considered that unlikely. Rose didn't seriously doubt that she'd eventually have placed me somewhere. Even so, the possibility of winding up in a government institution or orphanage did exist. Rose's point though was that whatever the outcome, she wouldn't have placed me with the Matthews family in East Kew. She made it clear that I would have been placed with a different kind of family. Now you can understand why she despised the system even though she was part of it.'

'A more "accepting" family,' exclaimed Colette. 'What on earth is that supposed to mean?'

'I guess a lower class family, at least in socio-economic terms,' I replied. 'You know how things were. A family not considered good enough to adopt a white baby but suitable to adopt a coloured one. Often Aboriginal kids were awarded to prospective adopting parents assessed as less than ideal. Kind of a booby prize so to speak.

'So you did the right thing in keeping quiet. No one would dispute that. I would never have had the opportunities that have come my way had you placed all the cards on the table back then.'

'What are you going to do, son?' enquired Vivian.

I didn't know. I had no idea whatsoever. The phone rang. Steven was calling from Chicago to finalise arrangements for his visit home to meet me.

CHAPTER 22

American Siblings

Next morning, a subdued Vivian kept very much to himself, keeping clear of the kitchen where Colette, Mark and I settled to chat. Eventually I approached him to find out what was going on.

'What's wrong, Vivian? You seem quiet today.'

'Oh nothing, I don't feel so good this morning son,' he replied.

'But why? What's happened?'

'I don't know if I can talk about it. No child should have had to suffer what we've done to you,' he commented sadly.

'But you haven't done anything to me. No one has done anything wrong. We're all cogs in a system. Don't worry, we'll survive. Things'll straighten themselves out. It's just going to take some time for me to decide what to do, that's all.'

After Vivian left for work, Colette and I chatted quietly until my mother headed off to do a few chores. Mark and I were left alone. 'Come on Mark, let's get out of here and go for a drive,' I suggested. 'I could do with some air. Why don't we check out a few Indian sites? Are you into that sort of thing?' I was delighted to learn that Mark did in fact share my interest in history, revealing a considerable knowledge of the county's Indian heritage. Heading out the door, we strode towards Mark's metallic blue '68 Pontiac Bonneville, a two-door Yank-tank which seemed to stretch forever. Never enamoured of large American cars, now I was confronted by one of the ugliest I'd ever laid eyes on — and it belonged to my new baby brother!

'Now that's a bitchin' machine, don't ya think?' beamed Mark with unrestrained pride. 'She's got a 400 cubic motor, bored 30 with a Holley four barrel.'

What that all meant escaped me entirely. Now, besides Peter the motor mechanic, I had another brother fanatical about cars!

Mark and I roamed far and wide during the course of my visit, cruising the linear roads which divided the corn country into uniform grids dormant during winter. It was driving around in this way that the two of us got to know each other.

Right from that first time on the phone, I'd been struck by the natural empathy between the two of us. My brother and I communicated with consummate ease. For Mark, there was something miraculous about my unexpected appearance and, like me, he was undergoing fundamental change. I was surprised to learn Mark enjoyed driving alone along deserted roads at night whenever he needed to think or unwind. I'd also done that since first learning to drive. But of course there were stark differences too. Like Peter, and unlike me, Mark was practical and gifted with his hands, painting houses during university breaks to support himself financially. His reputation conferred a steady flow of jobs.

The second night of my stay, Mark sidled up to me in the kitchen while Colette and Vivian chatted quietly in the television room. 'Something tells me you need a break, Gordon. What say we disappear for a while? We could go for a drive and stop for a beer. How does that sound?'

Although that was precisely what I felt like doing, I felt guilty about not spending my time with Colette and Vivian. We'd only known each other for forty-eight hours but Mark seemed to understand intuitively the pressure I was feeling. Was I that easy to fathom? 'What are you talking about?' I parried. 'I don't need a break.'

'Listen, don't give me that bullshit,' replied Mark kindly. 'For someone I met for the first time two days ago, I reckon I know you pretty well. Don't try to tell me you wouldn't mind poppin' out for a while because I know that you would.' He sidled over and placed his arm around my shoulder. 'Listen man, I understand what you're goin' through. You don't have to pretend with me. I'm on your side. Don't forget that.'

I gave in. 'OK, you're right, I could do with some time out.'

Mark smirked triumphantly. 'Well, relax then. There's nothin' wrong with that. Let's get goin'. I'll just tell the folks that we're poppin' out for a quick one, eh? We'll get back early. That way you'll be able to say goodnight before they head upstairs. I'm sure it'll be cool with them.' Mark's judgement proved spot on. Colette and Vivian didn't appear to mind at all, though I still felt guilty. I wondered if they genuinely weren't offended.

Clambering into the 'mean machine', we headed for the Chicken Coop, another student hangout. The Coop was more relaxed than Carol's, a different clientele entirely. Mark clearly felt more at ease here. Dress and image were unimportant. The setting stirred memories of my early teens. Tucked away in the corner, a local band churned out cover versions of Neil Young standards engraved indelibly on my mind. My brother and I downed Michelob Classic Darks and buffalo wings, and settled into our first serious conversation.

We talked first about Mark's girlfriend Sylvia, the local woman he would later marry whom I'd met that morning when she visited the house. Our encounter had verged on the farcical because, although Sylvia knew who I was and I understood that she did, the fact that I was Mark's brother was never explicitly acknowledged between us. Mark had told me that, unbeknown to his parents, he had explained my existence to her on first learning about me. Ridiculously in retrospect, the charade was maintained throughout my visit.

Mark was curious about my other family. A few of his questions made me feel extremely uncomfortable, especially when they related to Mum. I felt guilty talking about another mother. Mark obviously wasn't sure whether to refer to her as my mother or just plain Bell. 'How are you copin' with all of this?' he asked eventually. 'It must feel extraordinary. I only have to deal with one new family member, and that's difficult enough. You've got five of us to incorporate. I really don't know how ya do it. I can't begin to imagine what it must be like. I don't reckon I could handle somethin' like what you're havin' to manage as easily as you appear to be doin'.'

I remembered my brother's age, a mere twenty-one. How was he dealing with the turmoil he must have been experiencing? Youth made him especially vulnerable to our revised circumstances.

'How am I coping? Impossible to say Mark. The only thing that overwhelmed me like this was when Dad died nine years ago. At the moment I'm just trying to keep everything under control. Even though I'm physically here and we're doing what we're doing, in a way what's happening isn't sinking in. Everything's so unreal. One thing's for sure, I feel dramatically different from when I first arrived. It'll take ages for everything to settle down. Shit. I mean I've got to incorporate another family into my life and there's still Steven and Janet to meet. One down, two to go.'

Glancing at each other the two of us laughed nervously. 'You're right, it'll take a long time for everything to settle down,' Mark agreed.

Gradually as we talked on, the mood at the table darkened. Looking up I noticed Mark crying, tears streaming steadily down his cheeks. 'Hey mate. What's up?' I enquired. My brother continued weeping, reluctant to look up. 'Talk to me, will you? Talk to me,' I coaxed until, after wiping his face with his sleeve, his composure returned. I wrapped my arm around his shoulder.

'Oh, I don't know. I mean, what can I say?' spluttered Mark. 'I just feel incredibly sad, that's all.' Afraid our drama might be observed, I glanced around the bar. Thankfully, the Coop had swung into top gear, its inebriated clientele oblivious to the two of us. Now seemed an ideal time to disappear. Not to mention the possibility that some of Mark's university mates might turn up.

'Come on Mark, let's get out of here,' I suggested, the two of us rising simultaneously and heading for the door. Outside the wind whipped ferociously as we strode towards the 'bitchin' machine'.

Entering the car, Mark started sobbing again until I guided his face towards me. 'Come on Mark, talk to me will you? What's wrong? Please tell me. We have to work this out together. You're going to have to trust me. Remember, we're brothers now.'

Slowly Mark's tears receded. 'I don't know Gordon. I just feel incredibly sad that we never grew up together. I always wanted another elder brother. Steven and me get on fine, but we're different you know. With you, it's something else. I feel so comfortable. It's amazing how we seem to understand each other, don't you think? Why couldn't we have grown up together?'

'Listen Mark,' I responded. 'It is incredibly sad that we haven't been raised together. We've both been cheated of something. However, there's nothing we can do about what happened. We can't dwell on that now. The past can't be retrieved. We've got to look on the positive side and take things from there. I mean look what we've been given. Each of us has gained a brand new brother from another country. Think about that for a moment. How many people experience something as extraordinary as that?

'We've both been handed a special opportunity. In a way I can't believe my luck. Sure, we're different in heaps of ways and you don't know much about where I come from, that's for sure. Apart from that, I'm fifteen years older and not a mid-westerner.' Mark grinned. 'Differences are unimportant though,' I continued. What's important is not who we are as individuals but the fact that we're blood brothers from different countries thrown together for the very first time. How many people get to experience something like that? Provided we trust each other from the outset, everything will work out fine.'

Leaning towards each other, Mark and I embraced. The mood softened. 'I'm so pleased we've met, Gordon. I would have loved to have had a brother like you,' he repeated.

'What are you talking about? You have now,' I reminded him.

Unexpectedly a raucous mob of students passed by. Despite the chill, the car windows hadn't entirely frosted over. I wondered if they could make out the two of us hugging inside. The situation was extraordinary, and there was still Steven and Janet to go — and the matter of my Aboriginality to explain to all three.

A few days later, Steven arrived from Chicago. Unable to wangle more than a weekend plus a couple of days' leave, getting to know each other was going to be an intensive experience. A corporate sales executive servicing a clientele scattered throughout his midwest patch, Steven was out of town more often than not. I was intensely curious to meet my other brother, although the fragments I'd gleaned about him made me wonder whether or not the two of us would hit it off.

There were certain things we did share. Both of us were naturally garrulous, our mouths occasionally landing us in trouble, but generally proving a major asset. We also both attracted women. However, when it came to fundamental attitudes and values, my instincts warned me we were decidedly different. A staunch Republican Party supporter, Steven had served briefly in the army and was a committed reservist. I couldn't have been more different. My dislike for the Scotch College cadet corps and opposition later to the Vietnam war confirmed that.

Although we'd never actually laid eyes on each other, this wasn't our first encounter by any means. The two of us had already chatted on the phone and, as with Mark, I was captivated by Steven's midwest accent. It seemed incredible that I now possessed two brothers who sounded like that. Sometimes I'd phone just to savour their voices, Steven's speech less drawling and more confident than that of my youngest brother. The idea that we were actually flesh and blood was extraordinary.

Catching Steven at home alone generally proved difficult. On weekdays he left his apartment at dawn, not returning until late at night. Other than phoning him at the office — which I preferred to avoid — the only option was to catch him early in the morning, between when he woke and departed for work.

Steven's girlfriend Naomi, who sometimes stayed overnight with him, represented an additional complication. Steven had chosen not to mention my existence to her, at least not for the time being. In any case, the relationship was waning because, unlike Steven, Naomi was anxious to marry. Another consideration was that Naomi was adopted herself. Steven worried that mentioning me might prove unsettling for her.

So I would phone around six in the morning, hopeful he would be alone. Steven's tone revealed instantly whether or not he was able to talk. If Naomi was present, he would hang up, pretending that the caller had dialled a wrong number. On the occasions when a female voice did answer, it would be me who would ring off abruptly. During the months before Steven and I met, her boyfriend's early morning calls must have intrigued Naomi no end. I wondered if she suspected he was seeing someone else.

Anyhow, today we were going to meet. As Steven's arrival drew nearer, Colette busied herself in the kitchen preparing lunch. Under the pretext of obtaining supplies, Mark and I headed off to the supermarket. Our real purpose, however, was to get out of Colette's hair for a while. And despite my desire to meet Steven as soon as possible, I figured it might be easier for everyone if I wasn't around when he arrived. My absence meant he could chat with Colette and Vivian before my return.

On the way back home, I asked Mark repeatedly if he thought Steven might have arrived already. 'Settle down will ya,' ribbed Mark. 'I mean it's only another brother you're about to meet. Anyhow, you've already met the best one.' The two of us laughed. Turning into the street, Mark pointed ahead. 'Guess what? Looks like it's show time Gordo. That's Steven's car over there. One more brother coming up!' he chortled, as the Yank-tank wound into the drive and glided smoothly to a halt.

As we walked through the garage doorway which opened directly onto the inside hall, our mood sobered instantly. Turning towards the kitchen, I headed cautiously for Steven's voice, distinct and audible. A few more steps and he'd be visible.

Entering the kitchen, we found ourselves face to face. Steven appeared just as I'd expected from the family photos. The only difference was a moustache which made him seem somewhat older and more conservative. There was something about his face that recalled my travels on the Indian subcontinent. I imagined him seated opposite in the carriage of an Indian train.

My immediate instinct was that the two of us would get along fine. While apprehensive like me, Steven appeared genuinely delighted to see me. There was something about our meeting that recalled a first date, the same hushed air of expectancy and hopefulness that things would work out. We shook hands, then hugged.

Colette's lunch turned out to be a swish affair, a Thanksgiving re-run with a turkey and all the trimmings. After lunch, we all headed off to the cinema, Steven and I travelling together in his car. 'How do you really feel about all this Steven?' I asked. 'What do you think about my turning up?' As with Mark, I wondered how I would have felt had I been in my twenties and a brother appeared out of the blue. 'It must have come as one hell of a shock, eh?' I ventured. Steven glanced across uneasily. We were still sussing each other out.

'I guess I feel pretty weird,' he murmured eventually, tapping the steering wheel tensely as he spoke. 'I mean, it's real difficult to believe all this is goin' down. Do you know what I mean? Christ! Think about it. Here I am cruisin' down a highway next to an Australian brother I met for the first time a couple of hours ago. It's too crazy for words.' I understood precisely what he meant.

Mustering courage, I asked a question that was niggling away inside me. Embarrassed, I turned towards the window. 'Listen Steven, I need to ask you something important. I know we've only known each briefly, but I want to talk to you as a brother.' Steven appeared sheepish and uneasy. 'Do you think Colette and Vivian are genuinely happy about what's happened, about my turning up? They don't have any reservations or anything, do they? Tell me the truth.'

'Dad told me that he could die happy now,' Steven whispered seconds later, before breaking down. 'He said there was nothing more he wanted from life.'

My throat ached as tears welled inside and a sorrow too profound to articulate engulfed me. 'And what about you? How do you feel about me, Steven?' I asked. 'Are you pleased I'm here?' Imagining myself in my brother's place, I had no idea how I would have reacted to such upheaval. I had always wondered if I might have other brothers and sisters, but Steven and my other new siblings hadn't suspected anything. They'd all been caught unaware.

'Listen Gordon. Can you imagine what a shock this has been for the three of us,' he replied. 'I mean, can you get a handle on that? We hadn't the slightest inkling you might exist. Mum and Dad never breathed a word. Three months ago, there were three of us and now all of a sudden there's four. Not in my wildest dreams did I ever suspect that Mum and Dad had surrendered a baby.

'Now you've appeared Mum's over the moon. She's just so happy. It was incredible how things unfolded. I'll never forget that Thanksgiving. My overriding concern was to protect the family. As the eldest son, that was the first thing that occurred to me. I wasn't gonna let anyone hurt Mum, no matter what. You can understand that, can't you? You're the eldest in your family too, aren't you? You know what I mean?

'It's impossible to express what a shock all this has been,' he continued. 'I guess things'll settle down with time, at least that's what I keep tellin' myself. Anyhow, Mum and Dad are delighted beyond words and at the end of the day that's all that matters. All I care about is their happiness. As far as I'm concerned, you're part of the family now.'

With that, things lightened up. 'God, look at us, will you,' I said. 'Better get ourselves together. We're getting close now.'

Turning off the highway, we entered the asphalt car park which encircled the complex. Colette, Vivian and Mark pulled up alongside a few minutes later. What a pity Janet's not here, I mused. Her presence would have meant that after nearly forty years, Colette and Vivian would have had their entire family together for the first time. Chatting in the foyer, I was conscious we must have looked like any regular family attending a Saturday arvo flick.

That evening, Steven and I went out to eat together, heading for

Carol's, chicken wings and popcorn in mind. Unlike Mark, Steven was completely at home at Carol's where he'd spent countless evenings during his undergraduate days just a few years previously. Somehow Carol's, homecomings and fraternities, seemed inextricably linked, and, as a former Homecoming King runner-up and fraternity member, Steven understood the Carol's scene intimately.

Perched on a bar stool beside him, it struck me as incredible that I could find myself in a bar on the other side of the world next to a new blood brother, the barman oblivious to our family connection despite the physical similarities. Then again it wasn't all that surprising when considered from a stranger's perspective. After all, when I opened my mouth I was plainly a foreigner. Steven's accent defined him as local. Never in a million years would a stranger conclude that we might be brothers. That was completely impossible.

As the night wore on, I became increasingly convinced that Steven and I accepted one another as brothers without qualification, the same as with Mark. A genuine affection and empathy existed. Thus far, I had been extraordinarily lucky. Now only Janet remained to meet: two down, one to go.

Returning home mildly inebriated, Steven suggested we head for Chicago to spend his three remaining days of leave together alone. Unhesitatingly I agreed. It was essential we spend as much time together as possible if we were to bond as brothers.

The following morning we mentioned our decision to Colette and Vivian, explaining that getting away by ourselves was important. My natural parents understood.

There was of course a reason for desiring time alone with Steven. Despite the fact that I'd now discussed my Aboriginality with Colette and Vivian, I still hadn't breathed a word to any of the children. It had been difficult enough with their parents. Cruising around with Mark, I'd almost introduced the subject on numerous occasions, my courage invariably wilting. It was disturbing enough that the children's perceptions of their parents had already been upended. What would they think now when I explained my Aboriginality? I could scarcely begin to imagine, although then again they probably didn't even know what an Australian Aboriginal was. And having been raised in a society as racially diverse as the United States, would they even understand the sense of racial difference that had influenced and shaped me so strongly growing up in 1950s white, middle-class Australia?

Still I was concerned that explaining my Aboriginality might impinge adversely on their relationship with their parents once they understood how my unexplained race had affected my life. Would my new siblings understand why Colette had not explained my background at the time she surrendered me? How could they understand that in an Australian social context? And what would they think of the choices I had made? Would they understand and sympathise or would they judge harshly what I had done?

However they were going to react, it seemed ridiculous not to tell them the truth. They deserved to know precisely what had drawn me into their lives. No matter how much I wished to avoid it, it was crucial that they learn from me first-hand what had shaped my identity and how I had become Aboriginal. I felt desperate for their support.

That afternoon, Steven and I downed a few whiskies, our conversation increasingly melancholy with every charge. Again I found myself procrastinating over my tale.

'Steven, there's something I need to talk about. I've got a problem and I need your advice,' I ventured an hour or so later.

For the second time in less than a week, I found myself explaining how I'd become Aboriginal.

To my immense relief, Steven reacted calmly, seemingly taking what I explained in his stride. 'Wow. That's one helluva story, man. To think you've been through all that by yourself. That can't have been easy.' I could sense Steven considering what else he might add.

'Listen Gordon, given that you never knew your racial background, I can easily understand how all this developed,' he said eventually. 'Everyone else will too, if that's what you're worried about. Christ, you haven't done anything wrong. On the contrary. You should never have had to go through all this. Let me tell you somethin' which Mum and Dad don't even know. Vivian's colour also affected me when I was young. I had a hard time in primary school, with name callin' and so on. Occasionally I got into fights. Whenever my clothes were messed up during a scuffle at school, I'd sneak through the back door and into the bathroom to scrub up so that Mum wouldn't notice. I'm pretty sure she never did. She certainly never said anything.

'My situation was different though. At least I knew where I came from. I can't begin to imagine how not knowing must have felt, it must have been extremely difficult.' Listening to Steven's words, I felt indescribable gratitude. The fact that he understood my situation made me feel enormously privileged.

That evening, the two of us experienced a disturbingly close shave when, entirely by chance, we encountered one of Janet's close friends. Dining in a downtown bistro, Steven and I had barely finished ordering when my brother turned towards me ashen-faced. 'You're not going to believe this Gordon. I've just noticed one of Janet's college friends sitting over by the window and she's seen me. Shit, she's heading our way. What shall we do? Who in the hell am I going to say you are if she asks?'

Swept up in the panic, I forgot Mark's suggestion that we claim I was a cousin visiting from Australia. The two of us became increasingly agitated, Steven drawing on his cigarette while I fidgeted nervously. 'Stand up and talk to her,' I instructed. 'Go on. Move away from the table. I'll bury myself in the menu.'

Janet's friend strolled over towards us. Without looking up, I could feel her eyes on me. Steven advanced quickly towards her. They greeted each other midway across the room. The pressure unbearable, as I had done to escape the Canadian at Chicago airport, I retreated to the bathroom where I loitered until it seemed safe to return.

Rejoining Steven, I was relieved to see that Janet's friend had returned to her table. 'Thank God for that,' I sighed gratefully. 'How did it go? Tell me what she said. She didn't suspect anything?' Steven shook his head. 'I really didn't give her a chance,' he replied. 'I mentioned I was with a friend and quickly introduced another subject. She didn't enquire at all.'

I turned towards the the girl's table once again. She was studying me. My eyes returned to my recently arrived entree.

As we both calmed down, Steven and I discussed how best to handle any similar crisis. 'If something like this happens again, follow Mark's suggestion and say I'm a cousin visiting from Australia,' I suggested. 'That's foolproof. No one can dispute that.' But where I fitted within the family structure still required clarification. Would I be the son of Colette's younger sister who lived in Sydney and didn't even know I existed? Or might I be the child of a sibling of Vivian's we could claim had migrated to Australia? Vivian possessed two siblings, one in Sri Lanka and one in England. A brother and a sister. Either of these would explain my olive complexion. Then there was a third possibility; we could claim that Colette's sister had married a non-Anglo-Saxon, which could also explain my colour. Considering all three alternatives, the most credible explanation seemed to be that I was the son of one of Vivian's siblings who had migrated to Australia and married an Anglo-Saxon. I could improvise from there.

'Colette told me that in future, whenever people enquire, she's going to tell them that she has four children, not three,' I said to Steven. 'She's planning on handling things openly. Still, when it comes to the crunch, I wonder if she'll have the courage to do that. It will be incredibly hard to explain that kind of change, especially at her age. I don't know what the answer is, but things can't continue indefinitely as they are. Everything needs to be placed in the open and, whether I like it or not, that includes my Aboriginality.'

Steven nodded in agreement. 'You're right. Until this Aboriginal problem's resolved officially, you'll never be entirely free. This is going to wear you out or drive you crazy beforehand.' Steven wasn't telling me anything I didn't already know. I understood that precisely. Nevertheless, I had no idea whatsoever how I was going to rectify things. Extricating myself from the mess I was in appeared nigh impossible.

Of all my new family members, Janet was the one I felt most apprehensive about meeting. The image I had constructed was of an intelligent, disciplined, formidable character and I recalled vividly her initial hostile reaction to the bombshell of my existence. Since that time, Janet essentially hadn't spoken to her father, pointedly avoiding him for the remainder of her Thanksgiving stay and again over Christmas — the only two occasions on which she had travelled home since my appearance. Janet's relations with Colette were similarly frosty, although my sister did comunicate with her mother.

No matter how hard I tried, I simply couldn't understand Janet's behaviour. Unfamiliar with Australia in the 1950s and the social climate which her parents had confronted, my sister appeared unable or unwilling to understand their dilemma. The circumstances which forced her parents to give me up for adoption clearly lay beyond her grasp. That frustrated me intensely.

I also needed to establish precisely what it was that troubled her. Why the anger? Was it the fact that she'd been displaced as the eldest child? Did she feel perhaps that her parents had been less than honest? Was she ashamed that they had surrendered a child? Although it was impossible to arrive at any definitive explanation, I suspected that she was shocked that her mother had been forced to give up a child and that perhaps blame towards Vivian played a part.

Maybe it's more difficult for a daughter to accept the fact of her mother giving away a child than for a son, I reflected. After all, that's what the children's reactions seemed to suggest, contrary to what I would have anticipated. Steven and Mark had been generous with their hearts and entirely supportive. I had expected that Janet would be the one most sympathetic to her mother but ironically this did not appear to be the case. I wondered why Janet had been unable to find within her a similar compassion.

Another possibility was that Janet felt deceived and cheated — even excluded perhaps — because her parents had never revealed the fact of my birth before now. But it would have been pointless for Colette and Vivian to have done that. I recalled a comment Colette made early during my stay. 'I think things would have been very difficult for the children had you turned up during their formative years. I would have welcomed it, but it still would have been complicated for everyone.' What she said made complete sense to me. I tried to imagine how the children would have reacted; I couldn't. It was only my unexpected materialisation thirty-four years down the track that made an explanation necessary. To have explained earlier about a child presumably lost forever would have been pointless.

Steven and Mark suggested another explanation. According to them, Vivian had raised his only daughter strictly, Janet complying dutifully with her father's stringent standards of behaviour. A diligent student, of the three children Janet had proved the strongest performer academically and also the most disciplined. Determined to ensure that Janet didn't wind up single and pregnant, Vivian had kept close tabs on his daughter's social activities, especially in relation to the opposite sex. For her part, Janet had behaved impeccably and had been a role-model adolescent from a parental point of view.

Now my appearance on the scene had possibly shattered Janet's perception of her father. No longer could Vivian be perceived as flawless. Possibly Janet judged him a hypocrite.

Our long-awaited meeting took place on a Saturday afternoon in Ames. Janet was due to head back to Houston the following evening as, like Steven, she had a demanding work schedule which simply couldn't accommodate a longer visit. Devoted to her career, Janet moved widely around the country, providing advice to corporate clients on computer information systems.

One look at Janet confirmed what I had imagined. My sister had an unimaginative, conservative, corporate style. When she explained that she sometimes shopped for clothes in a store where you described the particular look you were after to assistants who systematically attired you, I wasn't surprised.

Physically, what struck me most about Janet was her skin. Like the rest of us, she'd been endowed with enviable olive skin. As with Steven and Mark, a general similarity in appearance was also evident between Janet and myself although, in my sister's case, it was difficult to define. There weren't many specific characteristics in common, though a stranger observing the two of us together would have deduced a family connection.

Our first meeting struck me as contrived and businesslike, the two of us settling into polite, though formal, conversation, both parties conscious of negotiating a new relationship as brother and sister. The situation reminded me of a diplomatic encounter with a perceptive interlocutor.

Despite the conversation warming up gradually, the spontaneous affection and acceptance evident between myself and my American brothers was absent. Perhaps she's reserved by nature, I told myself. Now knowing Vivian, that explanation seemed logical. When it came to temperament, Janet obviously possessed more of Vivian in her than either of her siblings, both of whom struck me as more like their mother in terms of their natures.

Janet's behaviour during her visit home didn't make things easier for anyone. My sister made no attempt to disguise her anger with her father, snapping at him for no apparent reason. How I wished she could restrain her feelings and accept what had transpired generously and with more compassion. After all, it was now three months since I had first made contact and still Janet wasn't talking to her father — a fact which disturbed all of us immensely. For now Vivian appeared to accept Janet's behaviour, allowing time for things to calm down, although the situation clearly caused him considerable distress.

Although each of us felt confident that Janet's attitude would eventually improve, it still tried everyone's patience. 'You're really getting under my skin,' snapped Mark during one of Janet's outbursts.

'Stay out of this, Mark. What's going on between me and Dad is none of your business,' growled Janet angrily.

'Now hang on a minute, sis!' retorted Mark. 'You seem to have a few things mixed up. There's enough happenin' around here without this sorta bullshit goin' down. Grow up, will ya.'

Brother and sister glared defiantly at one another. At that

moment I realised that even if Janet was in the wrong, standing up for herself against two forceful brothers throughout childhood must have been anything but easy. I winced recalling how often I had teased Fiona and Kay when the three of us were young.

That night, Janet and I headed off for a quiet dinner together. This was going to be our first and last opportunity to be alone and therefore a crucially important night for each of us. Janet selected an up-market restaurant, assuring me she would be able to claim the cost on expenses. Although I didn't say anything, no way was I going to allow my sister to pay for dinner on this, our night out together. What brother worth his salt would allow a younger sister to pick up the tab on an occasion like that? Rather than argue, I decided to remain silent and let things ride.

Entering the restaurant, the maitre d' approached instantly. 'Celebrating anything special? Perhaps a birthday or anniversary of some kind?' he enquired while steering us towards a vacant table. Janet and I glanced at each other, my sister struggling to suppress laughter in response to the question.

'Can you believe what he just asked?' she joked, the moment he disappeared. 'Are we celebrating something special? Imagine if we'd explained the truth.' The two of us chortled with laughter.

As the conversation unwound, some of my preconceptions about Janet's attitude to her parents and their situation were confirmed. My sister possessed no real sense of what had befallen Colette and Vivian back in Australia, failing either to acknowledge the predicament Colette had faced or else being unsympathetic towards it. Either way, her thinking was impossible to fathom. Why couldn't Janet understand why her parents hadn't been able to keep me? It was all so glaringly obvious. Why couldn't she be more sympathetic? Explaining again the appalling dilemma her parents had confronted, Janet remained unmoved. I felt intensely frustrated.

Interestingly, Janet was sympathetic when I explained my mistaken Aboriginal identity, like Steven, understanding completely why it preoccupied me. In fact it struck me as more than a touch peculiar that Janet could understand my Aboriginality more easily than she could what had happened to Colette and Vivian. Janet also sympathised with my concerns about how the Department might react, and the difficulties I would face in 'de-Aboriginalising' on my return home. Hearteningly, I also gained the impression that, like Steven, she wouldn't judge Colette adversely for not having explained my race.

By the end of the night, assessing how things were developing, I realised that clearly we did get along despite my difficulties with Janet's attitude to her parents. In many ways I shared more in common with my sister than I did with my two brothers. Janet also enjoyed books, the theatre and travel, and unlike either Steven or Mark, my sister had spent time abroad as an adult although, like them, she had not been motivated to visit Australia.

Now it seemed Janet's attitude towards both my arrival and her parents was slowly mellowing. I felt confident that the rest would be simply a question of time. We had made a constructive start.

Now having met my American brothers and sister, I realised comfortingly that I did respond to them as natural brothers and sister. There were many affinities including the sense of humour I shared with my brothers and the way in which we understood each other intuitively. There was also the gentleness and vulnerability which I shared with Mark; the social and people skills I shared with Steven; and the interest in learning and personal development which I shared with Janet.

My mind turned to Fiona, Kay and Peter, my other siblings with whom I didn't share a single gene in common. In contrast with my American family, we had grown up together, developing emotional ties attributable to having been raised together in the same household by common parents. When I thought about it, my heart convinced me that now I did possess two sets of siblings, both culturally different and undeniably distinct, but each family nonetheless. However, I realised also that a part of me remained on my own.

CHAPTER 23

_____

Where it all Began

Now I'd discovered Colette and Vivian, I wanted to learn everything I could about my natural parents. Their stories were central pillars of my own, integral additions to my identity. While we had discussed aspects of these stories on the phone, it was not until my visit that I was able to assimilate them.

During our time together in Iowa, Vivian explained how he had departed Ceylon as a seventeen-year-old in 1948, the year the country achieved independence from Britain and twenty-four years before it adopted a new republican constitution to become Sri Lanka. My father had not been forced abroad by persecution, war or famine, the classic themes of immigration.

In part because they spent virtually no time together which survived in his memory, Vivian knew only snippets about his father, Sextus. He did know, however, that Sextus had been educated at St Thomas's College, situated at Mount Lavinia, the popular beach resort skirting Colombo, favoured by well-to-do Sinhalese. Four years later in 1991, during my first visit to this country dangling pendant-like below India, I visited the Mount

Lavinia cemetery where, following cremation and the filling of ash pots, I observed powdered remains discarded crudely in garbage bins along with wizened flowers and other refuse.

With dark, brooding eyes the most captivating feature of a handsome and distinguished face, Sextus cut a familiar and popular figure about town. I had found myself transfixed by the striking sepia photograph Vivian possessed of his father, seated imposingly on a Victorian chair, a man of distinction and propriety. A man of destiny. An accomplished cricketer, Sextus also devoted energy to whisky and arak — the local alcoholic beverage distilled from fermented coconut. What was left over he bestowed upon his wife, Sharmini Jayasingha, a resilient woman and the mother of their three young children.

Driving home in his four-door Phanard convertible after the annual cricket match between St Thomas's and Royal College, Sextus's life ended in a car accident while he was still in his twenties. I imagined Sextus and his young friends carousing outrageously in the vehicle and wondered if the misadventure had occurred in the same year that Royal boys had paraded around a coffin containing Thomian ashes prior to the important match. Whatever the case, in the unclearest of circumstances, my paternal grandfather fell beneath his vehicle and was crushed mortally. During four short years of marriage, Sextus, who had inherited property heavily mortgaged by his father, was unable to re-establish the family assets, leaving his widow to raise three children and salvage the financial mess.

Vivian's mother, Sharmini, was the eldest daughter of Nalin, who started out as a cook on a paddah boat, a flat-bottomed cargo vessel. From this small beginning, Nalin developed a very successful business transporting boatloads of copra to Colombo to exchange for rice, chillies and other staples to vend along the inland waterways of Ceylon's south. When business flourished,

Nalin purchased coconut and rubber plantations, the substantial profits providing his talented brood with a first-class education.

After Sextus's death, Sharmini and the children lived with her father, by then a wiry, silver-haired gentleman who enjoyed smoking cheroots. Shortly afterwards, Vivian's only brother, Hiran, was sent to live with Nalin's childless sister, who later committed suicide in mysterious circumstances when an affair became known.

Vivian thrived on the household cuisine, especially 'hoppers', his favourite dish. Sometimes the retiring youngster assisted the cook to prepare the hoppers from riceflour which stood overnight with yeast and a small quantity of arak to induce fermentation. The arak was prepared from sweet-tasting sap collected daily by Tamil labourers who scaled coconut palms to obtain it. Vivian's favourite accompaniment to the hoppers was a sambal comprising grated coconut, white and green onions, and turmeric. Vivian would listen tirelessly to his grandfather's stories, savouring his hoppers.

At three and a half years of age, Vivian was sent to St Mary's boarding school at Kollupitya on the outskirts of Colombo, but after only six months there he was transferred to the Catholic village school at Marawila where he remained until turning six. I could picture my father journeying to school by bullock cart through the surrounding villages and coconut plantations. Vivian had already shown me the only photo he possessed of himself from his childhood, a beaming and confident young infant with a tiger tooth suspended from a chain around his neck, bracelets adorning his chubby wrists, seated on an elegant carved ebony table. Feasting on my father's descriptions, I conjured up the coconut trees of that distant childhood, the tangerine fruit and the breeze gently rustling the fronds as Vivian travelled contentedly to school through the still of morning, hopeful that classes would be conducted in the shade of a splendid mango — infinitely preferable to the dormitory-style rooms of the village school I would encounter sixty years later when, sentimentally, I retraced segments of my father's past.

Vivian later boarded at St Thomas's College, where his father had been educated, remaining until 1941 when the school was commandeered by South East Asia Command forces under Lord Mountbatten, operating from Kandy, in the country's central highlands. Because of its allegiance to Britain and the Allies, Ceylon's major ports became strategic to the war's Asian arena. This made them obvious Japanese targets. In 1942, in what Churchill reportedly believed to be the most perilous point of the war, in little more than a week 1000 Sri Lankan civilians and Allied troops died in a Japanese assault. Thankfully the British defence was victorious in what represented a critical defeat for the would-be invaders. However, the allied occupation meant yet another school for Vivian, this time Saint Sebastian's, a Christian Brothers college, where he completed his secondary education.

Sipping his coffee, Vivian explained that after matriculating he decided to pursue a veterinary career, obtaining a Ceylon government scholarship to undertake pre-veterinary studies in southern India at Loyola College in Madras. Racial tensions between the Sinhalese and the Tamils in Ceylon were irritating bilateral relations between Ceylon and India, the Ceylonese government demanding that Indian residents assume Ceylonese citizenship or leave, in part to curb Indian Tamils removing currency from the country. The Indian government retaliated by refusing to accept Ceylonese students. Consequently, on completion of his pre-veterinary studies, Vivian found himself unable to commence full veterinary studies as he had hoped.

Returning to Ceylon and determined to develop his veterinary credentials, Vivian gained employment at a hill country cattle station and also with a major veterinary hospital where he undertook routine laboratory work. Determined to train abroad, Vivian contacted veterinary schools in several countries, including Australia, to seek admission. However, with the war now over, most unfilled university places in Australia were reserved for former servicemen. As a last resort, Vivian contacted a penfriend of his sister's in Sydney, who succeeded in securing a university place for him in Melbourne, a number of years before Australia began to attract educated Ceylonese and decades before Melbourne's Sri Lankan burgher community grew to flourish ('burgher' in the Sri Lankan context refers to Sri Lankans descended from European colonists).

In subsequent years, other Ceylonese would be attracted by a poster of a fair, rosy-cheeked, young girl in a summer frock standing in a field of golden wheat, a bouquet of native flowers in one hand and a cuddly lamb tucked under her arm. 'Come to Sunny Australia', the poster beckoned.

After months of fruitlessly awaiting funds from another Ceylon government scholarship he had obtained to assist study in Australia, Vivian used a 6000 rupee family bequest to obtain standby passage on an air force seaplane which transported six passengers from the southern coastal town of Koggala to Singapore. Following a three-week wait and a sudden call, Vivian found himself perched in the plane's fuselage among wire-rope beds with only tea, coffee and a single slice of bread and jam to sustain him during a journey which was to last fourteen hours.

Possessing limited funds, Vivian stayed with a relative from the Indian state of Goa who assisted him in arranging his onward travel to Australia. Although passages were heavily booked, thanks to his relative possessing a connection at Thomas Cook, Vivian arranged to travel on the *Gorgon*, a 400-ton cargo vessel which also accepted paying passengers. Arriving in Fremantle, the immigration officer confiscated Vivian's passport for no apparent reason, returning it later without explanation. Familiar with the 'White Australia' policy, Vivian assumed a connection but judged it sensible not to enquire.

Since Federation in 1901, a 'White Australia' was one policy which virtually all non-indigenous Australians accepted. Indeed, the concept of White Australia was a cornerstone of national identity and a fundamental tenet of the Labor Party. Earlier colonial legislation restricting first the entry of Chinese and subsequently Indians, Japanese and other Asians was to be enshrined in one of the first legislative measures of the Australian Commonwealth parliament. This was the *Immigration Restriction Act 1901* which effectively prevented Asian immigration into Australia. After 1901, non-whites could only enter Australia on a temporary basis under a permit. Justifying the policy, the *Bulletin*, the mouthpiece of Australian nationalism, proclaimed in 1901 that:

It is impossible to have a large coloured alien population in the midst of a white population without a half-caste population growing up between the two. India proves that; would prove it much more conclusively only the white population isn't large enough to be a very extensive parent to the Eurasian mongrel. Spanish and Portugese America show it. The United States shows it. Queensland (by importing Pacific Island labour) shows it already to an alarming extent. And Australia thinks highly enough of its British and Irish descent to keep the race pure.

Attitudes towards the entry of 'coloured' foreigners into Australia did not change significantly until after the Second World War when, in 1947, the government relaxed many of the rigid restrictions on non-European entry and settlement that had existed since the Immigration Restriction Act. Presumably this facilitated Vivian's entry the following year, although the number of Asian students entering Australia remained small. Even though the White Australia policy was formally discarded in 1973, real change didn't arrive until several years later, when the Fraser Government opened Australia's door to significant numbers of Indo-Chinese refugees.

Vivian left Perth for Melbourne via Adelaide on the trans-continental train. He stayed at the YMCA in dormitory accom-modation for five shillings per night, and advertised in the Melbourne *Herald* for private board at two pounds ten shillings per month.

The only reply came from a Mrs Reid in the northern suburb of Pascoe Vale South and her husband, a Gallipoli veteran and tele-phone company employee who enjoyed spinning yarns about the Turks. Within five minutes of meeting the couple, Mrs Reid invited Vivian to move in and call them Mum and Dad. Mrs Reid was warm and generous, doting on Vivian like an adored son.

Vivian started veterinary science classes well after the com-mencement of the university year, enrolling in night classes throughout the winter to catch up. Mrs Reid always waited up until he returned home, dinner in the oven, a hot water bottle placed thoughtfully in his bed. In return for his board, Mrs Reid provided breakfast, a cut lunch, an evening meal, towels and linen, and did all his washing and ironing. During these winter months, she also ensured that her husband obtained enough wood to feed the chip heater in the living room. When Vivian paid his board the first time, Mrs Reid insisted on returning ten shillings.

His landlady's generosity constantly embarrassed Vivian until the Melbourne *Sun News-Pictorial* Sunball Competition provided him with an unexpected opportunity to express his gratitude. Every Monday, following the previous Saturday's Victorian Football League matches, the *Sun* would publish an action photo with the football deleted. Football fans would then attempt to mark with a cross on the competition photo the precise location of the ball in play. The closest entry was judged winner, the prize pool proportional to entry numbers. To his astonishment, Vivian won at his first attempt, receiving the gigantic sum of 550 pounds. He insisted Mrs Reid accept half this amount, and put aside twenty-five pounds for the family he stayed with when employed at the veterinary hospital in Ceylon, whose house had been destroyed by a flood.

The following year, Vivian changed from veterinary science to science and moved from Melbourne to Sydney where, after paying for food and lodging, he dedicated leftover funds to records by artists such as Glenn Miller, Artie Shaw and Patti Page. Particular favourites included Nat King Cole and postwar bands, especially Kay Kaper's. He also collected original demo discs by cover artists. It was this love for music that led him to Colette, employed as a record buyer in the music department of the downtown department store where the demo discs Vivian collected were available.

I had already learnt from our phone conversations that Colette was the elder of two daughters, the only children of Charles and Moira Darcy, and that her childhood had been a disrupted one. Her parents' marriage first broke up when Moira was pregnant with Colette, then revived and collapsed periodically until it disintegrated when Colette was nineteen years old. Never curbing a penchant for gambling, Charles Darcy was financially irrespons-ible. However, it was the temper which flared during arguments with his wife that Colette remembered more than anything, explosions during which she would attempt to protect her mother from her father's wrath. But her interventions only goaded her father further and she often cried herself to sleep. When Charles left for good, Moira, a dressmaker who supplemented her work with millinery and making silk flowers, moved into a Sydney apartment, while Colette took up residence in the boarding house in Burwood where she lived when first pregnant with me. Although trained as a secretary, Colette sought alternative employment, obtaining her position as a record buyer.

Vivian was attracted to the helpful young woman behind the counter and, after a dozen or so visits, mustered sufficient courage to invite her out. Their first date was in a Dutch restaurant at Potts Point, a world away from the ubiquitous tiled-roof bungalows which dominated suburban Sydney at the time. At the restaurant they were the only patrons; Vivian splashed out on two bottles of Heineken. I found myself wondering, as Vivian recounted that night, about the courage needed for a reticent young Ceylonese lad to ask a white Australian woman out. What had been running through my father's mind? Surely he contemplated rejection. And what did Colette think about Vivian at the time of his (presumably) unexpected approach? Had she ever thought about him seriously, or considered him attractive? Aware that my natural parents were both conservative and decidedly private, I chose not to question further at the time, assuming I could fill in details later. Nor did I seek information about the minutiae of their relationship and how relations between them had developed over time. Later I would regret my circumspection because, as relations between the three of us unfolded, I would find myself no longer in a position to ask.

In time, the relationship having become intimate, Colette began to feel unwell, so visited a doctor. My natural mother became visibly upset during this part of her story. Suspecting a kidney problem, the doctor prescribed a medication, advising that side-effects might include missing a period. It was only after several periods were missed that Colette returned to the doctor, this time informing him that she believed she might be pregnant. Unsympathetic, the doctor didn't want to know, suggesting instead that she could have a tumour and referring her elsewhere. Using a false name, Colette then consulted a doctor in Kings Cross who detected a heartbeat and confirmed she was four to five months pregnant.

Following anguished deliberation, Colette and Vivian decided on adoption. With Colette supporting her mother and Vivian studying without a salary or Australian residency, marriage didn't appear to be a realistic option. Not living at home made it easier for Colette to ensure that those central to her life, her mother and her sister, never detected her pregnancy although, as the pregnancy progressed, she did experience second thoughts, considering asking her sister if she might pretend that the baby was hers. Colette recalled with horror the ostracising of a single, pregnant woman at the local church..

Once again I found myself confronting unanswered questions which I was later to regret not having raised at the time. In particular I wondered what, if any, other reasons may have caused Colette and Vivian to decide not to marry when she was carrying me, given that they married subsequently. I also wondered if Vivian's colour had played a role. Clearly a relationship between a white girl and a coloured man would have been frowned on by many Australians back then. The option of abortion also crossed my mind. Was this an alternative which Colette ever considered seriously? That seemed unlikely, given that at that time they were difficult to organise, not to mention expensive, illegal and dangerous. Anyhow, after four or five months, it was already too late.

I also wondered how Moira, Colette's mother, might have felt at the time? Would she have considered Vivian's race a negative influence on her daughter's future or would she have been supportive of the relationship? There were also socio-economic considerations. I imagined it might have been easier for Colette to pursue a relationship with Vivian than for someone of higher social status. Had the two of them been financially secure, would they have made a different decision?

Naturally, I was fascinated by and hungry for every detail of Colette and Vivian's stories, particularly my natural mother's personal account of surrendering me for adoption — right from when the Kings Cross doctor confirmed her pregnancy through to returning from Melbourne without her baby, her secret intact. I imagine that, because recalling this episode provokes such pain, Colette has only provided me with the barest details. On those occasions when I raised it, she would tremble and break down.

But I did learn from Vivian that he wrote to the Reids in Melbourne who agreed to assist in practical terms, insufficient funds preventing him from accompanying Colette to Melbourne. I assumed the Reids helped Colette find the family with whom she stayed during the final stages of her pregnancy, and later wondered why Colette had not simply lodged with them.

I tried to picture Colette arriving at the Queen Vic, timid, afraid and self-conscious, and being referred to Auntie Rose who, in her capacity as social worker, would have provided information and assistance. No doubt the two of them spoke periodically during this final stage of my mother's pregnancy. Auntie Rose recalled Colette as a private and self-contained individual with her own network. During visits to the hospital's pre-natal clinic, women who had decided to surrender their babies for adoption were provided with a letter to hand to the hospital sister on their admission.

With regard to hospital process, Auntie Rose had explained how the women would be placed in one of the long open wards typical of the day, although each ward possessed a two-bedder for patients requiring tranquillity or special attention. To their relief, some women who were to relinquish their babies for adoption found themselves located in this room, provided a bed was available, although they were separated from other mothers, cruelly and more obviously, at certain other hospitals. In the wards, medical charts were coded, significant information highlighted in red, including notice of a medical problem or advice that a woman intended surrendering her child for adoption, to alert medical and nursing staff.

To minimise their trauma, Auntie Rose always referred to the women as Mrs, purchasing wedding bands on their behalf from suspicious shop assistants across the road at Coles. To complete this scenario of respectability, Rose would encourage the women to claim that their husbands were working interstate or in the country and have someone send them flowers. I never found out if Colette had asked Vivian or the Reids to arrange the same thing for her. Should the women wish to talk with Auntie Rose during their hospitalisation, conversations were conducted in her office, rather than in the wards themselves, in order to avoid undesired attention. If the women sought permission to see their babies, Auntie Rose would furnish them with a letter asking the ward sister to organise it.

Later, when I asked Auntie Rose, she was uncertain if Colette had ever seen me following my birth. While practices varied from hospital to hospital, at the Queen Vic relinquishing mothers and their newborn infants were separated immediately following the birth for a three-day period, in goodwill rather than as punishment, to help the mothers to adjust and face the prospect of seeing a child (should they so choose) they would subsequently surrender. Like other women, Colette had already been provided with a copy of the 'consent to adopt' form prior to my birth and was prevented legally from committing her child for adoption for a period of five days following my birth, although solicitors acting privately did obtain signatures within that period.

Alone in my room in Iowa, contemplating the process which Colette had faced, I found it impossible to conceive the devastation which my natural mother had faced.

Following her return to Sydney, Colette resumed her regular life, as well as possible, continuing her relationship with Vivian who, the year after my birth, completed his science degree at Sydney University, where he helped establish the International Club. Arriving in autumn of that same year, Vivian spent five months in Canberra undertaking practical work required for his degree. Completing his research, he returned to Sydney before starting post-graduate studies in biochemistry at the University of New Zealand. It was during this time he married Colette in Sydney. Both products of disrupted backgrounds, I wondered if my natural parents had found comfort in one another.

Once Vivian had his second degree, he and Colette travelled to Ceylon, remaining there for two years before Vivian obtained a scholarship to undertake further studies in the United States. They travelled with just five hundred American dollars, Colette by then pregnant with Janet, her second child, half a decade after my birth.

Regrettably, I still don't have a clear picture of my parents' first years in the United States although Colette did mention they had been extremely difficult financially. Following the successful completion of his doctorate, Vivian spent a number of years working on research for major corporations in various cities before moving to the public sector and later entering academia.

CHAPTER 24

Regrets

Farewelling Colette, Vivian and Mark at Des Moines airport sealed an important chapter in my life. All appeared to have gone extremely well, with Vivian and the children at least, and later I would receive a card from Janet in which she said that she genuinely liked and respected me and hoped to call me a close friend one day.

At Des Moines airport, Colette handed me an envelope. Her instruction not to open it until I boarded the plane reminded me of the note Mum had given me prior to my departure for Iowa. As the plane taxied away from the terminal I opened the envelope to find two letters. The first was from Colette.

5 March 1987

My Beloved Son,

These past few weeks have been a dream come true, and for that I thank you. I am so proud of all you've done and accomplished and I know you'll make a name for yourself in whatever area your talents take you.

From now on, I plan to do everything I can to make people aware of registries that can bring birth parents and children together. The other thing I can hardly wait to do is tell some friends about what has happened. I have a real need to be able to talk about you.

Return to Australia and do what you must do, knowing you have left a part of yourself in Iowa.

Thank God life will never be the same again. I look forward to what the future holds for all of us.

With love always,

Colette

The envelope also contained a cheque, to cover the cost of a Canberra–Iowa return airfare, plus a letter from Vivian.

Dear Gordon,

We are so grateful to you for having the interest, initiative and fortitude to find us — it truly is one of the most cherished occurrences of my life. I hope that as a family we have been able to dispel any fear, trepidation and reservations you may have had in meeting and visiting us. I want you to know that wherever we live, you have a home.

Regrets, misdeeds and shortcomings have and are no strangers. I have had plenty but the one that is of most concern to me is the stigma of colour that you inherited from me and the toll it took on you during your formative years. Please forgive me. The flip side of the coin though is that you have used this situation to develop into a determined and mature person. Your achievements speak louder than words. Your future plans are stimulating. I hope and pray that your 'colouring' won't be an impediment to realising your goals and dreams.

We thank God for the Matthews family that nurtured you. I shall be writing to Bell.

God bless you and keep you safe son.

Love Vivian

I discovered later that during my stay, Colette had also sent the following letter to Mum.

25 February 1987

Dear Bell

I was so touched by your card, photograph and curl from Gordon's first haircut. It is something I shall treasure always.
These past ten days have been a miracle, the highlight of my life and something I have dreamed of for the past thirty-four years.

My gratitude to you is very profound, and I can see the love and respect Gordon has for you.
I am so impressed and proud of all that he has done and accomplished, and know his gifts and life will touch many people.

I hope we will meet one day.

With love and gratitude,

Colette

Yet, as I settled into my seat on the plane that would once again place thousands of miles between me and my new family, I realised something had gone wrong in relation to Colette. There was no hint of it in her letter but I recognised that my visit had left her disappointed.

Stretched out on the flight, I confronted the fact, avoided until now, that I had not been as open and generous emotionally with my mother as I had wanted or she had hoped. I had baulked at offering my heart and found it confusing and uncomfortable to pinpoint why. The fact that I had not handled things better gnawed at me. I felt like turning the plane around and starting anew.

I realised that I had denied Colette's greatest need: the opportunity to spend time alone with me and to talk freely, to unburden herself and to purge more than three decades of grieving. In order to absolve herself, Colette had wanted to share the pain that had consumed her ever since surrendering me for adoption. But I had held her at a distance.

On the one occasion when Colette did explain tearfully how she had suffered, I was overcome by her sadness. Objectively I could understand what she had gone through and the devastating extent of her suffering. Colette was trying to deal with the pent up grief and guilt of thirty-four years. But when confronted with the reality of that, I found it insurmountably challenging. I had no idea what I could do to help. Colette was my mother, but she was also, in most respects, a complete stranger. I felt incapable, awkward and reserved in response to Colette's desperate desire for understanding.

Apart from that one occasion, I had avoided emotional conversations with Colette whenever possible. Each time I sensed her desire to talk with me as mother and son, I had steered the conversation in another direction or attempted to avoid it altogether.

Colette never alluded to my defensive behaviour but I knew she detected it and that it saddened her. I just prayed she understood my own confusion.

Alone for the first time in more than a week, I wondered whether my reaction was typical of other adoptees who had met their birth mothers. Were the majority of them also wracked by confusion and competing loyalties? I suspected many were.

During the period between first finding Colette and actually meeting her, my revised circumstances had not seemed to impose any significant problem because I had been protected by distance. I hadn't had to deal first-hand with incorporating another mother and father into my life.

In retrospect, I now realise that I was in a state of panic and shock at the time I first met Colette. 'But I've already got my mother,' I thought guiltily, while staring into the face of the woman who had given me life. That had been the most confronting moment I had ever experienced, although at that time I suppressed my panic, choosing to pretend it didn't exist.

When I first arrived, Colette and Vivian had suggested I phone home to Melbourne whenever I felt the need. On the second day I accepted their offer, calling Mum to say that I had arrived safely and explain how things were going. Mum had enquired about Colette and Vivian. 'They're wonderful people but you don't have to worry, you're my real mother,' I had whispered, desperate to allay the guilt I felt about where I was and what I was doing. Again I wondered what Mum really felt deep inside. At the same time I was also fearful that Colette might inadvertently overhear our conversation.

As my visit unfolded, I increasingly realised that whenever Colette was around I felt pressured, as if she sought something I was unable to provide. It struck me that this was a problem I experienced only with her. I had felt entirely at ease in the company of Vivian and my brothers and sister, certainly after initial barriers had been dismantled. I thought fondly about the delight evident on Vivian's face whenever Mark and I were together. The pleasure he derived from seeing his sons interact was undisguised. But the relationship between mother and son was different, infinitely more intimate and intense. Sometimes Colette had entered the living room while I chatted with Vivian but often she only stayed briefly. I realised ashamedly that she sensed I was maintaining a distance, and that she withdrew as a result.

Despite my efforts not to, I found myself comparing my two mothers, weighing up one against the other. On the one hand, Mum had mothered me all my life. But Colette had given me life. Did either woman possess stronger claims to me than the other? The question seemed ludicrous, but I couldn't dispel it. The two women at the heart of my existence were markedly different people. Mum's life had been blessed with opportunity and she had also inherited formidable strength and resilience. I had always thought of her as the strongest, yet also one of the most sensitive women I had ever met. I recalled someone suggesting once to Mum that it must have been extremely hard competing against men to forge a successful career in the forties and fifties. Mum had replied that she had never once thought in terms of rivalry with men. 'I never considered gender a barrier. I simply never thought about it. I was too busy getting on with things,' she had said.

Like Mum, Colette was also kind and gentle, but far more timid and controlled. On the other hand, one of her qualities which appealed to me most and which I shared was her thirst for adventure and new experiences. Colette especially loved Mexico, and the opportunity which travel there provided to learn Spanish. She was a woman who, despite not having received all the advantages which Mum had enjoyed while growing up, had travelled widely, pursuing an interesting and fulfilling life, one of which she might feel justifiably proud.

I found myself acutely anxious not to offend either of my mothers. For example, whenever I spoke to Colette and Vivian about Mum, I consciously referred to her as Bell rather than Mum and whenever I spoke to Mum about Colette and Vivian, I always referred to them by their Christian names, never as my mother and father or 'other parents'. Likewise, I would refer to Dad as Rodney in conversation with Colette and Vivian. I found myself preoccupied with not slipping up. It was a difficult and uncomfortable balancing act.

Several years later, awoken by a phone call from Mum in the Buenos Aires apartment where I was living, I was curious when, after a cheery hello, Mum told me she had a visitor who wished to speak to me. I was shocked to hear Colette on the line. Unbeknown to me, making only her fourth visit home to Australia in almost forty years, Colette had contacted Mum and asked if they could meet. Delighted, Mum had collected Colette at her city hotel and taken her home to chat over afternoon tea and show her around the house in which her son had grown up. I had found that phone call from the family home, which Colette explained later had been initiated by Mum, incredibly disturbing. Being confronted by my two mothers simultaneously overwhelmed me. It was like two separate and distinct worlds, each remote from the other, colliding. Months later, I still shuddered when I thought about it.

The fact that I possessed two fathers didn't disturb me nearly as much, perhaps because Dad had died almost a decade before I had discovered Vivian. Anyway, fathers are different to mothers. There's something inherently more intense about the relationship between mother and child.

Also, Vivian was easy to relate to. For whatever reason, I didn't feel pressure in his company. I imagined myself interacting with a sensible and affectionate elder brother and I enjoyed his boyish humour. I admired him a great deal. A dignified man, Vivian was someone who approached everything he did with unflinching commitment, an individual who had quietly earned his place in the world without blowing his own trumpet, despite an impressive litany of achievements. His only blemish in his own eyes had been my adoption, about which he felt profound and unrelenting regret. Taking me aside at the end of my first visit, Vivian told me that with my adoption he had relinquished his right to judge either me or my behaviour. I felt immense sadness hearing that, imagining him seeking forgiveness on the frequent occasions he attended church.

CHAPTER 25

De-Aboriginalising

It had been three months before my trip to Iowa that I had learnt I was of Sri Lankan and not Aboriginal descent, and it left central aspects of my life in tatters. Plagued by hopelessness at the time, I felt confined and was preoccupied with escape, particularly at work. I was under increasing pressure and extremely depressed and my work performance deteriorated dramatically.

During the months leading up to my Iowa visit, Geoffrey Forrester, my branch head, counselled me several times on the need to improve my performance. Geoffrey was irritated by my erratic behaviour, but I kept the reason for it to myself. In fact, I was deeply worried by the prospect of being promoted the following year — the year of bicentennial celebrations — in an Aboriginal capacity. No one, including Geoffrey, could have imagined that my objective was to do everything necessary to prevent such an outcome. In an early report on my performance, the concluding comment of my training course director had been, 'I regard him as among his few leading contemporaries in most areas of performance'. Now I found myself intentionally unravelling what had been a promising career. Frustrated and disappointed, Geoffrey eventually gave up altogether.

By the time I returned from Iowa in March 1987, life had become stressful to an intolerable degree. I felt a complete fraud. I worried about what indigenous and other friends would think. Surely they would all be stunned by my revelation. And how would my colleagues react if I informed the Department of my revised status?

My preoccupation with the Department's likely reaction bordered on the paranoid. 'What the Department thinks is irrelevant,' I assured myself unconvincingly. 'After all, you never intended pursuing a long-term public service career anyway.'

Desperately considering options, I found it impossible to decide what to do. Two clear choices seemed apparent. On the one hand, I could continue as if nothing had changed, ignoring the fact that I had discovered a whole new family and established the truth about my race. That way I would remain eligible for the advantages which would inevitably accrue as an Aboriginal diplomat. But that would involve a life of deception and lies.

Alternatively, I could plunge ahead and explain to the Department that I was no longer Aboriginal. That would mean losing access to benefits and forfeiting my Fulbright scholarship. More fundamentally, it would require me to go through the wrenching experience of a complete change of identity. I dreaded the thought of reinventing myself. In turmoil and unable to think clearly, it never occurred to me that people would understand if I just explained how things were. Instead, I procrastinated further, withdrawing even deeper into myself.

Life began to assume a nightmarish quality, impossible to manage. Some days I would find myself in an Aboriginal role within the Department, then speak to Colette and Vivian the very same evening. The pressure of not explaining what had happened was slowly tearing me apart. Six months after my return from Iowa I finaly decided to unburden myself.

Desperate for a dose of Mum's commonsense, I visited Melbourne to discuss my predicament. There was no question for her. 'Just tell them the truth and see how things fall into place,' she advised in her usual straightforward manner.

I argued back, not convinced that Mum appreciated the full extent of the possible fallout. 'My Aboriginal friends, think how disappointed they'll be. They'll feel so cheated! And the Department mightn't be able to do anything officially, but this isn't exactly going to boost my career,' I moaned.

As always, Mum provided unwavering support. How I envied her ability to manage crises. 'Listen darling, you haven't done anything wrong. Keep calm and think carefully about who in the Department you might tell first; that's important. Then get on with it quickly. As for your Aboriginal and Torres Strait Islander friends, you're just going to have to tell them the truth and see how they react. Everyone will understand. You'll see.'

Back in Canberra the following Monday, I prepared for the difficult task of what I came to describe as my 'de-Aboriginalising'. Thursday would be D-day I decided. On that day I would start telling the handful of people I wished to advise first. Provided I could contact them all, it would be over by Friday, and I could take stock of my situation over the weekend. As the first few days of the week rolled by, my anxiety became oppressive. I could feel the pressure building inside my head. I broke out in hives, which I was able to cover up everywhere except on my hands.

I decided to speak initially with Benny Mills, Australia's first Torres Strait Islander diplomat and a friend. Benny was on secondment to Foreign Affairs from the Department of Aboriginal Affairs, working in the Human Rights Section, part of the International Organisations Branch where I was placed at the time.

Most of the Torres Strait Islanders I knew socially in Canberra I'd met through Benny at the Sunday kupa-murris he organised to bring community members together. A colleague, friend and indigenous Australian, Benny was the obvious place to start.

Thursday rolled around far quicker than I would have liked. Mustering courage, hesitantly, I approached my friend. 'How's it all going Benny?' I enquired, attempting to sound casual.

'Good thanks mate. No complaints at all. How about you? What've you been up to?'

'I'm OK. Not much going on but there is something I need to talk to you about. I've got a small problem,' I told him.

'Nothing too bad, I hope,' said Benny, concern apparent in his voice. 'Sit down and fill me in.'

'That's what I want to do, but away from the office. I really want to talk privately. Would you be able to drop over for a drink after work?' I suggested.

'Sorry mate, but tonight's absolutely impossible,' replied Benny. 'I won't get out of here until seven and then I'm playing basketball. Afterwards I've arranged to see a mate down from Brisbane who I haven't touched base with yet. He's heading north again tomorrow, so there's no way I can put him off. Tonight's the only chance I'll get to see him. And I'm off to Sydney first thing in the morning for a human rights seminar. Sorry, but this evening's not a goer. Why don't we talk over the weekend?'

I must have looked devastated. 'What's going on mate? Is this something serious?' Benny became alarmed. 'You're not sick are you? Come on, tell me what's up,' he persisted, irritated by my unwillingness to provide the vaguest hint. But I couldn't start to explain without unburdening myself completely.

'All right then,' Benny relented finally, 'I guess we can talk after I've finished basketball and seen my mate. It'll be late though,' he warned. That was irrelevant as far as I was concerned. All that mattered was that Benny would listen. We agreed that I should visit around midnight. Benny would be home by then, his wife Yvonne presumably sleeping.

Driving over to Benny's, the idea of our impending conversation terrified me. 'No point in procrastinating,' I told myself. 'Just get on with it and give it to him straight.'

Plonking ourselves down on opposite sides of a table, Benny picked at some food, waiting for whatever it was I was about to announce.

'Listen Benny, God knows what you're going to think, but I've discovered I'm not Aboriginal,' I blurted. A flicker crossed Benny's face then vanished. He appeared stunned, listening silently as I explained the massive impact on my life of having grown up without my race. Benny was especially understanding when I explained the confusion it had caused me when younger and how I had come to believe I was of Aboriginal descent and accept a formal Aboriginal identity when it was offered. We also talked in detail about the experience of meeting my American family for the first time and how momentous and redefining that had been.

Benny was overwhelmed. 'I can't believe what you've just told me. That's absolutely amazing,' he muttered, struggling to assimilate the bombshell he had just received. 'You must have been under a hell of a lot of pressure for an awfully long time,' he added, visibly moved. 'Anyhow, you don't have to worry. We won't allow anything to happen to you. I'll assist with this. I reckon you need a rest.' A wave of relief swept over me. Benny was going to help.

Next morning I woke early, preoccupied with the conversation I was planning to have later in the day with my branch head, Geoffrey. Despite his irritation with me and my less than distinguished performance at work, I felt he liked me and would be willing to explain my case to others.

Physically and emotionally exhausted with stress, I decided to phone Geoffrey early in the morning and tell him I was sick. At the same time I would arrange to talk with him later in the day. 'Morning, Geoffrey. It's me here,' I announced when he answered.

'And where might you be?' he asked sarcastically.

'I'm at home sick,' I replied. 'Sorry. I won't be in today.'

'Don't give me that, Gordon. You're not really sick. Not so sick that you can't make it in to work. Get yourself in here. There's heaps on.'

'Listen Geoffrey, I've got a problem and I really need your help. Could we talk today? Don't ask me what it's about because I don't want to get into it over the phone. I need to talk in person, ideally here at home. Could you possibly drop over at lunchtime?'

'Gordon I don't know what's on your mind, but I haven't got time to scratch myself today. My program's chockablock.'

'Geoffrey, you can't imagine how important this is for me. I've got to talk today.' Mystified by my behaviour, eventually Geoffrey agreed to drop by on his way home.

I awaited his arrival with steadily mounting anxiety. Finally I was about to reveal everything to the Department. This was the conversation I'd especially dreaded.

When he arrived, the two of us seated ourselves at the kitchen table, Geoffrey commenting on artefacts I'd collected in Nigeria. As with Benny, I mentioned straightaway that I'd discovered I wasn't Aboriginal. I was interrupted a few minutes later. 'Listen Gordon, before you go any further, I just want you to know one thing. Although I'm amazed, as far as I'm concerned it doesn't really matter whether you're Aboriginal or not. Do you under-stand? At the end of the day your racial background is of secondary importance. I'm interested in Gordon Matthews, the person, whom I happen to like. Whether you're Aboriginal or Sri Lankan is irrelevant.'

I went on, my branch head listening silently until I mentioned my family in the States. 'Now I understand,' Geoffrey interrupted, recalling my holidays in North America earlier in the year. 'It all falls into place. You've visited them already, haven't you?'

Our conversation turned to the possible consequences of my situation. 'What do you think will happen to me from a career point of view?' I enquired despondently.

'Oh, I think you'll survive,' reassured Geoffrey. 'After all you were recruited as part of the normal diplomatic intake, not because you were Aboriginal. We'll just have to juggle your status, won't we? Swap you from Aboriginal to Eurasian in the system,' he joked. 'However, we need to think about how we're going to manage things. For the time being I don't think many people need to know. Leave it with me and we'll talk again tomorrow. I want to think about this carefully.'

Farewelling Geoffrey, I felt a degree of relief I hadn't experienced in ages. Finally I could see light at the end of the tunnel. The following morning, Geoffrey suggested that for the time being only the senior officer in charge of management and personnel need know of my changed circumstances.

At this point in time, the only other people I wanted to tell were Jirra Moore and another Aboriginal friend in the Department, Veronica Tippett. I spoke first to Veronica who administered the Aboriginal and Torres Strait Islander Cultural Relations Program. Over lunch I explained everything in detail. 'Listen Gordon, I rolled around all night thinking about what happened to you,' she confided next day in the office. 'To think you went through all of that alone. I think that's absolutely shocking. I also feel incredibly sad. You're special to all of us. I feel a bit like we've lost a member of the family.' I struggled not to cry.

Jirra, Australia's first Aboriginal diplomatic passport holder, was posted in Bangkok at the time and therefore impossible to meet in person. I could have phoned but I decided to wait until he returned on leave. The two of us would be able to sit down quietly and chat. Jirra's partner Lorraine, with whom I also spoke after speaking to Benny and Geoffrey, agreed entirely.

A few months later, when Jirra landed back in town, I revealed everything to a spellbound listener. Like Benny, Jirra flinched when I mentioned I wasn't Aboriginal but said nothing until I finished. 'That's an incredible story mate, absolutely incredible,' declared Jirra when I finished. 'You must be thrilled with what you've discovered even though I can't believe you're no longer Aboriginal. That's terrible from our point of view. You belong to the team.'

'But what on earth is the community going to think?' I asked hesitantly.

'That won't be a problem,' Jirra reassured. 'Listen mate, this has only happened because of your extraordinary circumstances. It's as simple as that. Everyone's gonna see that. No one with a heart will think any different. Gordon your status may have changed, but you'll always be one of us.

'Ya know mate, your story reminds me of incidents I saw at Wreck Bay growing up, of relatives and others stolen from their parents. Your natural parents suffered in the same way as us blackfellas because of the era in which you were born. The system didn't allow your mother to keep ya. Archie Roach sings about it, "Torn from their mothers breast, said it was for the best, then took them away".

'It also reminds me of a day I was in the car outside a milk bar at Huskisson, not far from the mission. A young Koori friend was with me. The two of us had just finished collectin' oysters from the rocks. We headed into town to get a cold drink before returning to Wreck. As we chatted, a blue Range Rover driven by a young Aboriginal fella pulled up. His pretty white adoptive sister was with 'im. I knew the girl was this bloke's sister and not his girlfriend like I knew a lot of other things about 'im. More than he did 'imself.

'This bloke was one of our mob, one of the stolen kids. They took 'im, his sister and another brother away from their mother and adopted 'em out to a white family when they were extremely young. I can remember their mother screamin' as the welfare people left. I don't think he was ever told anythin' about his Aboriginal background. Shockin', eh?

'Now listen carefully,' Jirra continued, his tone increasingly confidential. 'You're not gonna believe this. Although I didn't know everything, I did know for a fact that this fella in the Range Rover was the brother of my Aboriginal mate sittin' right beside me. He'd been taken when my mate was young. My mate wouldn't have even remembered, although he knew he had other brothers and sisters who'd been removed. Back then the stolen boy was known as Paul Stevens. Just think, there was my mate sittin' only a few yards from his blood brother and he didn't even know. I didn't have the heart to say anythin' to him there and then. Still haven't, although maybe I should. There's somethin' incredibly sad about that, don't ya reckon?'

All I could think about were the similarities between this story and my own. Like me, the bloke in the Range Rover had been robbed of his race. In my case, twice.

Over the months I informed other friends. Like Benny, all were stunned by what they heard, especially those who, like many Departmental colleagues, had only ever known me as Aboriginal. Everyone sympathised with what I'd experienced, some weeping openly as I talked. But it was childhood friends who were especially intrigued to finally learn my complete story, solving a mystery which had intrigued them for decades.

There weren't many practical changes to everyday life. In no sense did my revised status impact adversely on my relationships with indigenous friends and acquaintances. They treated me the same as before. We still visited one another's homes and indigenous officers in the Department insisted I continue to participate in the informal group we had established to discuss issues relevant to indigenous staff.

However, sometimes I found the mechanics of change difficult. After all, you don't just announce to all and sundry that your racial status has suddenly shifted. It was something I told people selectively over an extended period of time. I was acutely conscious that some individuals believed I was Aboriginal while others now knew I was not.

During one conversation with a senior Aboriginal leader around this time, he suggested that I was still Aboriginal. 'No I'm not,' I responded.

'Yes you are,' he insisted. 'If that's what you've always thought you were then that's what you are. Your identity doesn't suddenly change.' That much was true. I had lived and been shaped by my assumption that I was Aboriginal. That identity was irrevocably a part of me.

'But no, I know I'm not Aboriginal any more,' I had countered nonetheless, Vivian firmly in mind. Maintaining that I was still Aboriginal would be like denying his existence. I couldn't do that now. In terms of my race, I had discovered the truth. That ghost had been laid to rest, although I realised that possibly for the rest of my life I would be reconciling the discoveries of my search with the assumptions of my youth.

I thought about what it meant to know that my father was Sri Lankan. Having believed that I was Aboriginal, it felt disappointing and anti-climactic to acquire a racial background that I had never anticipated. There was no sense of excitement or completion. Before arriving at the belief I was Aboriginal, of the nationalities I had considered I could be, Sri Lankan had figured, but only marginally, suggested by others on a mere handful of occasions. Given my interest in South Asia and background in Indian studies, it had been an ironic and curious discovery. And although at the time I discovered Vivian's heritage I had never visited his homeland, I did four years later and was constantly confounded by the fact that no one ever suspected my Sinhalese origins. On the few occasions that I did mention my background, it attracted surprise. But while discovering a Sri Lankan background didn't affect me emotionally, not being Aboriginal did.

Emotionally part of me was still definitely Aboriginal. Although I was now Gordon Matthews, Sri Lankan adoptee, my connection with Aboriginal Australia continued and wouldn't suddenly wither and die. Aboriginality was something of which I had been aware virtually as far back as my memory stretched. I had experienced first-hand what it felt like to grow up Aboriginal in mainstream Australia, albeit on distinct and unusual terms. I knew about discrimination towards indigenous Australians. I had suffered that. Like any fundamental experience, you don't unlearn that.

In my predicament, with so much to reconcile on a personal level, I thought often about the more general issue of reconciliation between indigenous and non-indigenous Australians. At the national level, reconciliation was increasingly prominent although it would be several years before it fully penetrated the mainstream with the federal government's launch of the formal process of reconciliation, aimed at finding a way for all Australians to share the country as equals.

I think it was the bicentennial march in Sydney on Australia Day the following year that raised reconciliation as an issue, entering the psyche of the average white Australian for the first time. As Sydney Harbour resounded with cheers for the First Fleet re-enactment, another celebration of historical significance was occurring on the fringe of the city centre: the largest march ever by representatives of the oldest race on earth. Travelling from places as distant as the Kimberleys and Cape York for this one special day, members of tribes from all around the country were represented. For me, two centuries of European settlement paled into insignificance, set against the evidence of at least four hundred centuries of indigenous presence in Australia. It seemed incredible that people who had occupied this country for that amount of time had been disenfranchised following European settlement, until 1967.

Arriving at Hyde Park to the cheers of thousands of supporters, a thunderous roar erupted as tens of thousands of peaceful protesters stretching several kilometres arrived at their final destination. The atmosphere was electric as the leaders wound into the park, a banner declaring 'Veterans of the 200 year war want peace and justice' unfurled proudly in front of them.

'There is nothing so finely perceived and so finally felt as injustice'; 'Our land, our life'; 'Forty thousand years of dreaming, 200 years of nightmares'; 'We will not forget, we will not go away, we will not be silent, we will not die, we will fight and we will survive', proclaimed others.

This was a veteran's march of a different kind. 'Today the Aboriginal nation has marched through the streets of Sydney,' march organiser, the Reverend Charles Harris, said later.

An eerie din of clapsticks, didgeridoos and tribal chanting rose above ochre-painted tribesmen, absurdly incongruous with the Mirage jet fighters which roared over the harbour as non-indigenous Australia conducted another distinct and separate celebration.

At the end of the day, however, what really resonated for me were the words of Galarrwuy Yunupingu, chairman of the

Northern Land Council, who concluded his address to the crowd with a message of reconciliation:

'We hope to establish a future for Australia, and that future is very simple and clear — white Australia together with Aboriginal Australians, and then we are all Australians.'

CHAPTER 26

Trying Again

Exactly one year after my initial visit, I returned to Iowa. While a crucial start, my first visit had left much ground uncovered with my new family, only so much could be achieved in less than two weeks with five new family members to incorporate. In particular, I was uneasy about the way my relationship with Colette had started. Unfortunately, the fact that I had mistakenly claimed an Aboriginal identity still troubled me to the extent that it cast a shadow over everything else at the time. Despite believing that I'd done nothing wrong, I found myself burdened with guilt and emotionally exhausted, my confidence devastated. I arrived erupting with frustration and anger over my situation. In that frame of mind, the visit was doomed from the start.

Colette and Vivian couldn't understand what was bothering me. Frequently irritable, I was impatient and abrupt in conversation. Why had life inflicted such complications on me? Other people's lives were more straightforward. Who else had to deal with a complete shift in their racial background and identity? For fifteen years I had claimed to be something which I was not and now I was having to deal with the consequences of that on different levels, with friends and family, with the Aboriginal community, in the workplace and, most confrontingly of all, within myself. Confused, resentful and unable to think clearly, I felt as if the ground had dissolved beneath me.

Colette bore the brunt of this frustration and anger. I found myself avoiding her far more frequently, snapping irritably at her on some occasions and responding abruptly when she did talk to me. I also said unkind words. I was lashing out but I wasn't sure at what. Maybe, deep down, the relinquished child in me blamed her for creating my racial predicament, by not having provided my background at the time of my birth before giving me away. Perhaps that resentment was the fount of my anger. Now, many years later, that seems the most plausible explanation for my behaviour, although at the time, on a conscious level, I denied it vigorously.

I remembered a television interview I'd seen with the American singer Eartha Kitt, in which she'd described herself as a bastard of mixed-blood whose mother had given her away. It struck me that those defining characteristics of our lives were identical, although more significant for me was the fact that I had been left to grow up without my race.

My behaviour during my second stay wasn't unrelievedly atrocious. I did make an effort during the latter part of my visit when, overcome by remorse and determined to rectify things before my departure, I suggested to Colette that we visit a nearby historical town in order to spend time alone together. Driving along, Colette explained tearfully her nightmare of relinquishing me while I listened silently. Whenever grief overwhelmed her and she burst into tears, her voice choking, I offered comfort as best I could with supportive words and touch. However, I was still unable to break through the unconscious barrier of my resentment and the fundamental tension between us remained unresolved. At the end of the drive neither she nor I felt forgiven or absolved. The day proved a dismal failure.

Unfortunately my problems with Colette began to change my relationship with Vivian. I had hurt her and this tainted Vivian's attitude towards me; in his restraint I sensed great disappointment.

I also realised during this visit that my relationship with Colette defined my relationship with my brothers and sisters. Their overriding concern was Colette's well-being. Provided she was content then I was welcome by all. During one of our drives, Mark said he noticed I preferred spending time with him than with Colette. He was right. Time spent with a younger brother was less emotionally pressured. During the few days spent with my other brother at the end of my visit, Steven also remarked on my relationship with our mother not progressing smoothly. Although he didn't say more than that, he was plainly disappointed. Not wanting to admit to my brother my turmoil whenever Colette was around, I declined to offer any explanation. In fact, I couldn't even explain it to myself.

During my visit I also made a short visit to New York to spend time with Janet, who'd moved there from Houston. I was staggered by the change I encountered. Thankfully, relations between Janet and Colette and Vivian had quickly returned to normal after my visit the year before, Janet apologising for her initial reaction to news of my existence and subsequent behaviour. She had come to accept the circumstances surrounding my birth and the way her parents had reacted.

Following a year to adjust to the fact of my existence, I found Janet relaxed, friendly and happy to have me around and a part of the family. At this stage, as far as I knew, she was unaware of my problems with Colette and the consequent tension in our relationship. I was struck more than on my first visit by how much we did in fact share in common, our bond strengthening during the time we spent together. Janet also told me that she couldn't believe how alike physically Vivian and I were, noting oddly the similarity in the shape of our torsos and forearms. It saddened me that at this stage of life, living separate lives in far-flung places, the opportunity to bond fully as brothers and sister was probably lost forever, despite the fact that we appeared to have become much closer.

A year later, I began my second posting, this time to Argentina, a country I had visited several times on leave during my time in Nigeria. In Buenos Aires I lived in an apartment in the upmarket Recoleta district of the Argentine capital, close to where Eva Peron lay buried amid the obscenely extravagant mausoleums with which the Argentine aristocracy immortalise themselves. It was also near a major cultural centre where I arranged the first ever exhibitions in South America of Australian Aboriginal painters. Despite no longer being Aboriginal, I still involved myself in the community and remained keen to promote Aboriginal culture whenever possible.

Settling into Buenos Aires, my thoughts turned frequently towards my family in the United States and my unresolved and deteriorating relationship with Colette following my discovery of her two years earlier. It was a dreadful thing, to have discovered another mother on the other side of the world, yet to have such a divide develop between us, due largely to me. So I decided to try once more, to invite Colette and Vivian to come to Argentina. I still couldn't put my finger on what the problem was, but I wanted to establish a meaningful relationship with them both. I was determined to make things work. I hoped a third meeting, the first on my territory, would give me a chance to draw us together emotionally, in the way I felt a long lost child and natural parents should be able to relate. I would take leave and the three of us could travel around the country. That would provide an ideal opportunity to enjoy what had been lacking until now, a relaxed and extended period of time together to mend fences with Colette. I was optimistic that Colette and Vivian would be willing to visit, provided Vivian could arrange the necessary time. By then, he was engaged in regular consultancy work following his retirement several years earlier.

I wondered if people would notice a family connection between the three of us and if we would be prepared to admit our relationship openly should anyone ask. Although I was, I doubted that Colette and Vivian were. In the letter I received at the end of my first visit, Colette had said she had a real need to talk about me and that she planned to do everything possible to make people aware of registries that unite natural parents and relinquished children. In fact, Colette had attended an adoption meeting in Chicago where she explained her story before a sympathetic audience. But as far as I knew there had been no follow-up. More than a year down the track, my sense was that Colette and Vivian had told virtually no one about me. Perhaps Colette's disappointment with me played a part. All the same, I felt frustrated that they still hadn't mentioned their first child to close relatives in Australia, England and Sri Lanka, all of whom I hoped eventually to meet. It seemed ridiculous that I'd seen photos of them — including Vivian's sari-clad sister who lived in Sri Lanka and two good-looking English cousins, Vivian's brother's children — but that they didn't even know I existed.

Shortly after my arrival in Buenos Aires, I was required to explain my story to the ambassador when, in the belief I was Aboriginal, the Department's director of public affairs in Canberra had suggested to a journalist planning a visit to Argentina that she write an article about me. When the director was informed by personnel that I was no longer formally Aboriginal, he phoned the ambassador to advise that he had made a *faux pas*, and warn that the journalist would probably contact the embassy. At the time the ambassador explained this, I filled him in on my story.

'Are you going to explain openly who they are?' asked the ambassador when I first mentioned that my natural parents proposed to visit.

'I'm not quite sure,' I replied. 'It's a bit tricky, it'll depend on circumstances and who we run in to.'

Colette and Vivian arrived in October 1991. Waiting for them at the airport, I felt apprehensive but hopeful. This was my chance to redeem myself with Colette. When they arrived, Vivian appeared strained from the journey. Despite his clean living, he had experienced health problems and aged noticeably in the three years since I'd last seen him.

On the second day of their visit I organised a dinner at home with several friends, Alejandro and Virginia, an Argentine couple whose son was my godchild, and an Australian journalist friend from Canberra, Don, then based in Buenos Aires. This was an important occasion for me, the first time ever I would have Colette and Vivian together with friends in my home, but it would reveal how complicated things could get if everything wasn't out in the open.

The day of the dinner a woman phoned me, coincidentally an acquaintance of a Sri Lankan friend who lived in Melbourne. He had provided the woman with my number, her only contact in Buenos Aires. The woman suggested we meet that same evening, which couldn't have been less convenient. Still, I invited her, telling my other guests beforehand that this person would be the only one present unaware of Colette and Vivian's true identity. Later I would wonder why we never just explained, but somehow we judged the occasion too special to warrant including a stranger in our confidence.

As my Argentine friends entered the apartment, for the first time I found myself saying, 'I'd like you to meet Colette and Vivian, my parents.' It was a weird, redefining experience. Everything progressed smoothly until Colette visited the bathroom during dinner. 'I'm having such a nice time chatting with your Mum,' Virginia blabbed, a trifle inebriated. Vivian was busy in conversation and didn't hear. The Australian woman glanced across but said nothing until after dinner when, finding the two of us alone, she enquired if Colette was my mother.

'It's a complicated story,' I responded dismissively. 'How about I fill you in another time?'

'Sure,' she replied, her curiosity undiminished. What concerned me most about that episode was the absurdity of not being completely open and honest in my own home.

After my guests departed and Colette and Vivian retired to bed, my mind returned to that first morning in Iowa when Colette had asked Mark who he would say I was if we ran into classmates on the university campus. I also recalled my dinner with Steven in Chicago, and the drama our encounter with Janet's friend had caused. I had recognised then that everything would need to be aired openly sooner rather than later. The realisation that, for whatever reason, that time had still not arrived disappointed me immensely, far more than the incidental fact that my dinner guest did not know Colette was my mother.

During Colette and Vivian's stay the three of us travelled widely including to the Iguazu Falls on the border of Argentina, Brazil and Paraguay, to Ushuaia, the world's southernmost town, and to several other places in Tierra del Fuego. While we enjoyed travelling together — except for the occasion when I skidded on gravel and ran our hire car off the road — and on the surface everything appeared to progress smoothly, the tension in my relationship with Colette continued unabated. We both still felt nervous and uncomfortable whenever we were alone with one another. There was a barrier between us which we were unable to understand or dismantle. With an honesty that has sadly only arrived with hindsight, I now see that the obstacle was on my side.

Time and again I debated with myself as to why I could not relax emotionally with Colette. Was it my difficulty with the idea of two mothers? Or unconsciously was I still angry that I had grown up without my race? What was responsible for this unintentional but chasmic divide between us? I realised I was incapable of fathoming precisely what the problem was and considered seeking professional advice although I never did.

During the second week of Colette and Vivian's stay, a further irritant surfaced in our relationship: my increasing preoccupation with writing a book. During my first visit we had all agreed that I had an important story to tell. Most importantly though, I felt that writing a book would enable me to place my difficult journey in perspective and to move ahead with my life. Ever since hearing it, a number of journalist friends and professional writers had encouraged me to try to put it down on paper. I had finally decided to do so.

What I wanted to say went much wider than my own story. I hoped that reading about what I had experienced might provoke people to think about the range of social issues involved: the plight of the several hundred thousand Australian women who had relinquished children for adoption; the situation of adoptees; the effects of racism and the circumstances of indigenous Australians. If I could write something which could enhance public awareness of these issues, even in the most humble way, then I wanted to try.

Originally I had told Colette and Vivian that I might attempt to write a novel. Thinking about it, I realised that my story would have greater impact if told directly and honestly. A fictionalised account would diminish its impact, and in any case I wasn't a novelist.

When I mentioned to Colette and Vivian that I had reconsidered how I wanted to tell my story, explaining that I now favoured a non-fiction account, they were disappointed and upset. Despite my repeated assurances, they feared a true account would threaten their privacy and anonymity.

Discussing my problems with Don, my journalist friend, I realised that my natural parents and I had fundamentally different perspectives on our 'rediscovery'. My need was to explain myself. By comparison, Colette and Vivian wanted to deal with what had occurred discreetly and in private. We were pulling in opposite directions.

Don's view was that Colette and Vivian were ecstatic that I had appeared in their lives, but that they might still feel guilty that they had given me away, not to mention having burdened me with my racial complication. He wondered if they were worried about being judged and thought that was a strong possibility. Even though the social values of the day were to blame and not my parents, it was possibly difficult for them to have sufficient confidence that others would understand.

Whether Don's analysis was right or wrong, at the end of our three weeks together little had changed. My mind returned to my anxious wait at Ezieza aiport, thirty kilometres from the city centre, when my parents had first arrived. My relationship with Colette had dominated my thoughts as I awaited her appearance in the arrival hall. It did as she departed. But now the distance between us had widened.

CHAPTER 27

Lock Out

In the months immediately following Colette and Vivian's visit, contact between us became less frequent, ceasing entirely following an acrimonious telephone conversation during which I had asked them if they ever mentioned me to anyone. I was upset to hear that Colette had not even revealed my existence to her only sister who was married with children and lived in Sydney. True, Colette and her sister were not overly close, but Colette had actually come to Australia, had visited Mum, and still not seen fit to tell her only sister that she had a nephew. She told me she had chosen not to broach the subject in view of our 'unresolved relationship'. Frustrated and angry, I had hung up. Despite thinking about Colette and Vivian constantly, it would be three years before we next spoke and, during those years, I often tossed restlessly at night, guilty and frustrated over how our relationship had broken down.

Rationally I knew that Colette and Vivian's situation was undoubtedly difficult for people of their age and generation. It would be extremely uncomfortable for them to introduce a new,

previously unheard of child into their public life, especially in the
conservative and in many ways parochial midwest where they had
settled due to Vivian's career. Word would quickly get around, the
story might become distorted, and people would inevitably
gossip. Possibly the whole community would end up knowing,
including individuals Colette and Vivian would prefer did not.
They were obviously concerned about what others might think
and unwilling to have their painful secret revealed openly.
Although I could see all of that, I was deeply hurt that they felt
unable to acknowledge me.

It occurred to me that perhaps I had already alienated Colette
irreversibly; that we had passed the point of no return. Her heart
had been brimming with joy at the time we had first met. But I had
hurt her unintentionally as a result of being burdened with
problems. Yet again it struck me that in part the reason had been
my difficulty with coping with the idea of two mothers. Perhaps I
thought so highly of Bell that no one else, not even a natural
mother, could compete or rival her importance and pivotal role in
my life. But that wasn't the fundamental problem. I realised that
the real culprit had been my racial problem and the angst and
confusion that had caused. As I had acknowledged at the time,
that had been all-consuming and overshadowed everything,
swamping entirely the experience of discovering and meeting
natural parents.

Rather than encountering a relaxed and carefree son, Colette
had been confronted by my anger, frustration and obsessive self-
preoccupation. I could understand how she had ceased to fully
trust me. I had wounded her, perhaps to an irreparable degree.

It struck me that it would likely appear extraordinary to an
outsider that Colette and I should get so close yet never actually
establish fully a genuine mother–son relationship. Had the racial
problem not been part of the equation, I felt certain that our

relationship would have unfolded entirely differently. Realising that made me immeasurably sad.

Perhaps now it was simply too late for us to develop the bond which in the depth of our hearts we both still yearned for. Only time would tell. Maybe insurmountable pain and resentment resided in each of our souls. That also remained to be seen. Although I was still keen, I understood that it would be difficult to start afresh.

In early 1995, I re-established contact, sending a conciliatory letter to Colette and Vivian to which they responded offering to meet me half way. I was relieved to learn that like me they wanted to repair the damage to our relationship. However, we didn't speak again until my birthday in June that year when, having recently circulated my manuscript to several publishers, the publisher with whom I eventually signed, phoned me at work out of the blue to tell me that she had read the first chapters of my book and was interested. During our conversation, the message light on my phone lit up. Clearing the call I was staggered to find it was Colette calling from Iowa to wish me a happy birthday. That evening, before I was able to phone back, Colette and Vivian called me at home, Colette assuring me that she wanted to resurrect our relationship. I said that I did too and that her phone call was the best birthday present I could possibly have received.

The day after my birthday I received a letter from Vivian in which he said:

I believe firm relationships are made when the parties concerned bring with them mutual respect, an ability to see and understand all aspects of the situation, and the compassion to forgive after listening to each other honestly and openly. You are our flesh and blood and we are ready to reach out to you to the same extent that you reach out to us.

Our thoughts and prayers are with you on your 43rd birthday. We
hope the day and the year that follows brings you the fulfilment of
your wishes, dreams and plans. You are and have been a part of us.

Later in the year I wrote a detailed and intimate letter to Colette
and Vivian which explained all aspects of my project, including
that I had found a publisher, and stressed how important it was to
me to obtain their support. I emphasised the cathartic nature of
what I was doing, and that with my book's publication, I would
finally purge my demons. Conscious of the need to involve them
fully, I suggested that I visit so that we could discuss things in
person. In concluding my letter, I told them that I prayed they
would support me and that, most importantly, we would now be
able to move ahead together as parents and son.

I waited anxiously, uncertain how Colette and Vivian would
respond. The reply I received couldn't have been more disappointing. They wanted no part of the book, and lacked any confidence
that I would protect their privacy. The letter also advised that the
dates I suggested for a visit were inconvenient, but declined to
suggest an alternative timing. Almost a decade after first finding
them, we were now further apart than ever. I felt hopelessly
locked out.

CHAPTER 28

Reconciliation

I am now forty-three years old and by the normal yardsticks — job, friends, income, health — leading a comfortable, interesting and successful life. Outwardly, I would appear to be extremely blessed. At a deeper level though, there is much to mourn. Ten years after my search began, I am still a long way from finding my own happy ending.

Almost miraculously, I found my natural mother — and father, brothers and a sister; my own blood kin. I found them, but only to lose them again. So where, and to whom, do I belong? Undoubtedly, a huge part of me belongs with Mum and my adoptive family, whose genes I do not share, but who were and remain a real family to me in every sense of the word, despite our considerable differences. Threads of my spirit are woven in different places but this was the environment in which I was raised, the environment which shaped me, and which undoubtedly influenced me more than any other.

Even though relations remain ruptured at this point in time, part of me also belongs with my family in the United States, despite cultural differences and a life spent separately until a decade ago. Although we met under extraordinary and difficult circumstances, which had a disastrous impact on how our relationship unfolded, I believe my story is not yet complete — certainly that's my hope. At the bottom line, we are flesh and blood. Colette and Vivian gave me life.

While in a sense I am the product of two families, two worlds, there also remains a part of me which is unique, something that I treasure as mine. It is the legacy of my confused origins and my sense since childhood of being apart and on my own.

As for the Aboriginal community, I am grateful to them for giving me a race. Familiar with dispossession, they recognise and accept generously the dispossessed. To them I owe a race which I embraced and which seemed to embrace me. As it turned out, I was wrong about my race. Yet for a while I had what I needed most: a complete sense of identity, a place in the world, a community where I belonged and to which I contributed.

I wonder if it is better to have belonged and been wrong than never to have belonged at all? The answer to that is an unequivocal yes. The identity which I acquired conferred a great deal that was positive and that will remain with me forever: friends, community and culture. Aboriginal Australia will forever own a place in my heart.

However, there was an enormous downside to having claimed Aboriginality. I can never adequately put into words the anguish and torment which accompanied my discovery that for a decade and a half I had inadvertantly claimed the wrong race. Readjusting to new circumstances has proved incredibly stressful, and led to the seed of my new relationship with Colette and the rest of my American family falling on barren ground. Had I never become an Aboriginal, there would undoubtedly have been far less angst and confusion and, most likely, a successful relationship with my natural family.

I have asked myself if I would ever have started my search had I known where it would end. Finding a new family and reinventing much of my life has proved wrenching in every sense. And despite the fairytale beginning to our relationship, the point that Colette, Vivian and I have now arrived at could scarcely be more disappointing. That is the saddest thing of all, the failure of my union with a new family.

Has the truth been worth the pain? I know in my heart it has. At thirty-four years of age, I learnt for the first time precisely who I am. Coming to terms with that was tough, but I think it is fair to say I approached the challenge with some courage, honesty and determination. I feel proud of that. My mystery solved, I might have hoped for a greater sense of peace, yet this remains elusive.

At journey's end, what preoccupies me is Colette. She has been the true loser in my story, surrendering a child she never wanted to relinquish, grieving constantly for thirty-four years before his reappearance, only to have her dreams dashed when he is unable to give his heart and the forgiveness she deserves. For now, the status of that so often glorified relationship between mother and child in our case remains unclear. Colette and I have not completed our journey.

As I conclude my book and try to banish my ghosts, I am hopeful that the barriers dividing me from my natural family can be breached. This book has been in part an effort to bridge the gap between us, but I have been only partially successful, as much as I feel that a weight has been lifted from my shoulders. And there is no denying the truth that emerges from these pages: I will not be at peace until Colette and I achieve our own reconciliation.

Bibliography

Ellis, V.R. (1981) *Trucanini Queen or Traitor,* Australian Institute of Aboriginal Studies, Canberra.

Horton, D. (general editor) (1994) *Encyclopaedia of Aboriginal Australia*, Aboriginal Studies Press, Canberra.

Mulvaney, D.J. (1969) *The Prehistory of Australia*, Thames & Hudson, London.

Parbury, N. (1986) *Survival — A History of Aboriginal Life in New South Wales*, Ministry of Aboriginal Affairs (NSW), Sydney.

Stanner, W.E.H. (1968) *After the Dreaming, The Boyer Lectures*, Australian Broadcasting Commission, Sydney.

Wasson, V.P. (1939) *The Chosen Baby,* J.B. Lippincott Company, Philadelphia.